Living Meaningfully,
Dying Joyfully

Also by Geshe Kelsang Gyatso

Meaningful to Behold
Clear Light of Bliss
Buddhism: A Beginner's Guide
Heart of Wisdom
Universal Compassion
The Meditation Handbook
Joyful Path of Good Fortune
Guide to Dakini Land
The Bodhisattva Vow
Heart Jewel
Great Treasury of Merit
Introduction to Buddhism
Understanding the Mind
Tantric Grounds and Paths
Ocean of Nectar
Essence of Vajrayana

Tharpa Publications is a publisher of Buddhist books that provide the most complete and integrated presentation of the Buddhist path to enlightenment available in any western language, from basic introductions to Buddhism and meditation to detailed and lucid expositions of the highest Buddhist philosophy and Tantric practice. There is a Tharpa website at www.tharpa.com.

GESHE KELSANG GYATSO

———

Living Meaningfully, Dying Joyfully

THE PROFOUND PRACTICE OF TRANSFERENCE OF CONSCIOUSNESS

THARPA PUBLICATIONS
London

First published in 1999

The right of Geshe Kelsang Gyatso
to be identified as author of this work
has been asserted by him in accordance with
the Copyright, Designs, and Patents Act 1988.

Tharpa Publications
15 Bendemeer Road
London SW15 1JX

Cover painting of Buddha Avalokiteshvara
by Chating Jamyang Lama.
Cover design by Stefan Killen.
Cover photo of Geshe Kelsang by René Knopfel.
Line illustrations by Andy Weber and Ani Kelsang Wangchen.

British Library Cataloguing in Publication Data
A catalogue record for this book is
available from the British Library.

ISBN 0 948006 64 1 – papercase
ISBN 0 948006 63 3 – paperback

Set in Palatino by Tharpa Publications.
Printed on acid-free 250-year longlife paper and bound
by Butler and Tanner, Frome, Somerset, England.

Contents

Illustrations

Acknowledgements

This book, *Living Meaningfully, Dying Joyfully*, gives a full, practical explanation of the Mahayana Buddhist practice of transference of consciousness, known in Tibetan as 'powa'.

The text was drafted by the author during an intensive editing retreat during the winter of 1998/99. We humbly thank Venerable Geshe Kelsang Gyatso for his inexhaustible kindness in conceiving and preparing this text for the benefit of contemporary Buddhist practitioners. In undertaking this work the author once again demonstrates his own great qualities of wisdom and compassion, knowledge and experience.

We would also like to thank all the dedicated senior Dharma students who worked with the author to edit the book and prepare it for publication.

Roy Tyson,
Administrative Director,
Manjushri Mahayana
Buddhist Centre,
May 1999.

Buddha Shakyamuni

Introduction

There is nothing more precious than our human life. Having been born as a human being we have immense freedom to accomplish almost anything we want. We can become a powerful politician, a successful businessman or woman, or a great scientist or artist. We can travel the world or even go to the moon, or we can settle for a simple family life. With so much freedom, we need to ask ourself what is the most meaningful way to use our life. What will make us truly happy? What will benefit others most? And when this life is over, what will help us then?

If we ask ourself these questions sincerely and deeply we shall discover that the way to make our life truly meaningful is to dedicate it to spiritual development. In essence this means to eliminate our negative and deluded states of mind, and to cultivate positive, peaceful states. By making this our priority, the negative minds that are the source of all our problems, such as anger, jealousy, attachment, pride, and ignorance, will gradually decrease; and our positive qualities, such as love, compassion, and wisdom, will increase. As a result we shall enjoy a happy, peaceful life, free from anxiety and problems, and we shall naturally benefit others. Spiritual practice is what gives meaning to our lives, and by applying our practice at the time of death we can die joyfully and experience pure, lasting happiness in all our future lives. Eventually we shall be able to transcend all the limitations of ordinary existence and attain the highest state of all, full enlightenment.

If we do not keep death in mind throughout our life, when the time of our death comes we shall suddenly discover

1

that all our wealth and possessions, and our friends and relatives cannot help us. Since we have not built up an inner strength through spiritual practice we shall feel intense regret for having wasted our life, as well as fear of what will happen during and after our death. Our tears and cries for help will be too late. We shall be like Mondrol Chödak, a Tibetan greatly admired by all who knew him for his many worldly skills and talents. He led a very full life, travelling from place to place and meeting many people, but when his death suddenly came he cried out: 'I have done so much, engaged in so many business ventures and so many worldly activities, but not one of these will be of any use to me now. People say that I am very clever but in fact I am incredibly stupid because I have completely neglected spiritual practice, which is the only thing that can help me at this time. I have wasted my whole life by doing things that are of no real benefit.' He felt strong regret and wept, and in this miserable state of mind he passed away.

Dying with regrets like this is not at all unusual. To avoid such a sad and meaningless end to our life we need to remember continually that we too must die. Contemplating our own death will inspire us to use our life wisely by developing the inner refuge of spiritual realizations; otherwise we shall have no ability to protect ourself from the sufferings of death and what lies beyond. Moreover, when someone close to us is dying, such as a parent or friend, we shall be powerless to help them because we shall not know how; and we shall experience sadness and frustration at our inability to be of genuine help. Preparing for death is one of the kindest and wisest things we can do for both ourself and others.

The fact of the matter is that this world is not our home. We are travellers, passing through. We came from our previous life, and in a few years, or a few days, we shall move on to our next life. We entered this world empty-handed and alone, and we shall leave empty-handed and alone. Everything we have accumulated in this life, including our very body, will be left behind. All that we can take with us from one life to the next are the imprints of the positive and negative actions we have created. If we ignore death we shall waste our life working for things that we shall only have to leave behind, creating many negative actions in the process and having to travel on to our next life with nothing but a heavy burden of negative karma.

On the other hand, if we base our life on a realistic awareness of our mortality we shall regard our spiritual development as far more important than the attainments of this world, and we shall view our time in this world principally as an opportunity to cultivate positive minds such as patience, love, compassion, and wisdom. Motivated by these virtuous minds we shall perform many positive actions, thereby creating the cause for future happiness. When the time of our death comes we shall be able to pass away without fear or regret, our mind empowered by the virtuous karma we have created.

The Kadampa Teachers say that there is no use in being afraid when we are on our deathbed and about to die; the time to fear death is while we are young. Most people do the reverse. While they are young they think 'I shall not die', and they live recklessly without concern for death; but when death comes they are terrified. If we develop fear of death right now, we shall use our life meaningfully by engaging in virtuous actions and avoiding non-virtuous actions, thus creating the cause to take a fortunate rebirth. When death actually comes we shall feel like a child returning to the home of its parents, and pass away joyfully, without fear. We shall become like Longdöl Lama, a Tibetan Buddhist Master who lived to a great old age. When the time of his death came he was overjoyed. People asked him why he was so happy and he replied 'If I die this morning I shall be born again this evening in a Pure Land. My future life will be far superior to this one.' Longdöl Lama had prepared carefully for his death and chosen the

3

specific place of his rebirth. If we use our life to engage purely in spiritual practice we can do the same.

Although intellectually we all know that one day we shall die, generally we are so reluctant to think of our death that this knowledge does not touch our hearts, and we live our life as if we were going to be in this world forever. As a result the things of this world – such as material possessions, reputation, popularity, and the pleasures of the senses – become of paramount importance, so we devote almost all our time and energy to obtaining them and engage in many negative actions for their sake. We are so preoccupied with the concerns of this life that there is little room in our mind for genuine spiritual practice. When the time of death actually arrives we discover that by having ignored death all our life we are completely unprepared.

What is death? Death is the cessation of the connection between our mind and our body. Most people believe that death takes place when the heart stops beating; but this does not mean that the person has died, because his subtle mind may still remain in his body. Death occurs when the subtle consciousness finally leaves the body to go to the next life. Our body is like a guesthouse and our mind like the guest; when we die our mind has to leave this body and enter the body of our next rebirth, like a guest leaving one guesthouse and travelling to another.

The mind is neither physical, nor a by-product of purely physical processes, but is a formless continuum that is a separate entity from the body. When the body disintegrates at death the mind does not cease. Although our superficial conscious mind ceases, it does so by dissolving into a deeper level of consciousness, the very subtle mind; and the continuum of the very subtle mind has no beginning and no end. It is this mind which, when thoroughly purified, transforms into the omniscient mind of a Buddha.

'Buddha' is Sanskrit for 'Awakened One' – one who has awakened from the sleep of ignorance and is free from the dream of mistaken appearance. Since beginningless time sentient beings like ourself have been trapped in the night-mare of samsara because we have never woken from the sleep of ignorance, not realizing that all our suffering is just the creation of our own confused mind. It is only through gaining realizations of Buddha's teachings, which are known as 'Dharma', that we are able to wake up from this dream-like samsaric suffering. These realizations are our real inner protection from suffering. Those who have gained Dharma realizations are known as 'Sangha', and they form the spiri-tual community who help us in our spiritual practice and set a good example for us to follow. Because they are so precious, Buddha, Dharma, and Sangha are known as the 'Three Jewels'.

Buddha said that every action we perform leaves an imprint on our very subtle mind, and each imprint eventually gives rise to its own effect. Our mind is like a field, and perform-ing actions is like sowing seeds in that field. Virtuous, or positive, actions sow seeds of future happiness and non-virtuous, or negative, actions sow seeds of future suffering. The seeds we have sown in the past remain dormant until the conditions necessary for their ripening come together. In some cases this can be many lifetimes after the original action was performed.

The seeds that ripen when we die are very important because they determine what kind of rebirth we shall take. Which particular seed ripens at death depends upon the state of mind in which we die. If we die with a peaceful mind, this will stimulate a virtuous seed and we shall experience a fortunate rebirth; but if we die with a dis-turbed mind, in a state of anger, say, this will stimulate a non-virtuous seed and we shall experience an unfortunate rebirth. This is similar to the way in which nightmares arise from our being in an agitated state just before falling asleep.

The analogy of falling asleep is not accidental, for the process of sleep, dreaming, and waking closely resembles the process of death, intermediate state, and rebirth. As we fall asleep, the inner energy winds that support our gross minds gather and dissolve inwards. As a result our mind becomes progressively more and more subtle until it transforms into the very subtle mind of the clear light of sleep. While the clear light of sleep is manifest we experience deep sleep, and to others we resemble a person who has died. When it ends, our mind becomes gradually more and more gross and we pass through the various levels of the dream state. Finally, our normal powers of memory and mental control are restored and we wake up. When this happens our dream world disappears and the ordinary world of our waking state appears.

A very similar process occurs when we die. As we die, our energy winds dissolve inwards and our mind becomes progressively more and more subtle until the very subtle mind of the clear light of death manifests. The experience of the clear light of death is very similar to the experience of deep sleep. After the clear light of death has ceased we experience the stages of the intermediate state, or 'bardo' in Tibetan, which is a dream-like state that occurs between death and rebirth. After a few days or weeks the intermediate state ends and we take rebirth. Just as when we wake from sleep the dream world disappears and we perceive the world of the waking state, so when we take rebirth the appearances of the intermediate state cease and the world of our next life appears.

The only significant difference between the process of sleep, dreaming, and waking and the process of death, intermediate state, and rebirth is that after the clear light of sleep has ceased the connection between our mind and our present body remains intact, whereas after the clear light of death this is broken.

While we are in the intermediate state we experience different visions that arise from the karmic seeds that were activated immediately before death. If negative seeds were

6

activated these visions will be nightmarish, but if positive seeds were activated they will be predominantly pleasant. In either case, once the karmic seeds have matured sufficiently they impel us to take rebirth in the lower or higher realms of samsara.

When we think of death we tend to think of it as something that happens to other people, but in reality, of course, sooner or later we too shall die. The time of our death is completely uncertain; there is no guarantee that we shall not die today. When by carefully contemplating the above explanation we understand clearly the existence of our future lives, we shall realize that future lives are endless. We shall then see that the happiness of future lives is far more important than the happiness of this life, and that the suffering of future lives is far worse. No matter how much suffering we may experience in this life, it is still only the suffering of one single life and its duration is very short – like a dream that quickly passes. On the other hand, since our future lives are countless, the potential suffering of those lives is endless, and if we do nothing to prevent our future suffering now it will last forever. If we think deeply about this we shall recognize the importance of not wasting our precious human life and of engaging in the spiritual practices that will prepare us for our death.

All living beings have two basic wishes – to be happy all the time, and to be completely free from suffering and problems. We can fulfil these wishes by following the instructions presented in this book. Through sincerely practising these instructions we can transcend our ordinary life and make genuine spiritual progress, and we can even attain the highest state of full enlightenment. Furthermore, if we apply these instructions as we are dying we shall die joyfully and experience permanent happiness throughout all our future lives.

PART ONE

Practising Powa to Benefit Ourself and Others

Buddha Complete Subduer with
the Essence of Vajra

Buddha Jewel of
Radiant Light

Buddha Powerful
King of the Nagas

The Preliminary Practices

What is 'powa', or 'transference of consciousness'? Powa is a method by which accomplished meditators transfer their consciousness to a higher rebirth. At the time of death our mind naturally leaves the body but generally cannot choose its next rebirth. Experienced practitioners of powa, however, can choose their next rebirth and direct their consciousness to a higher state at the time of death.

The practice of powa was first taught by Buddha Vajradhara in Tantric texts such as *Vajradaka Tantra*, *Little Sambara Tantra*, and *Sambuddha Tantra*. Various Indian Buddhist Masters relied upon these sources for their powa practice, and the Mahasiddha Naropa explained a special practice of powa in his *Six Yogas*. Powa later flourished widely in Tibet, and a living tradition of these teachings still exists to this day.

Buddha taught powa practice for those who have not entered the path to liberation, or for those who have accumulated many non-virtuous actions. By practising powa sincerely they can avoid rebirth in the lower realms and transfer their consciousness to the Pure Land of a Buddha; and this is true even for those who formerly led an evil or reckless life.

In a Buddha's Pure Land everything is pure; there are no sufferings, no contaminated environments, and no impure enjoyments. Beings born there are free from sickness, ageing, poverty, war, harm from fire, water, earth, and wind, and so forth. They have the ability to control their death and rebirth, and they experience physical and mental

11

suppleness throughout their life. Just being there naturally gives rise to a deep experience of bliss. Moreover, everyone living in a Pure Land has the opportunity to receive teachings and blessings directly from the Buddha of that Pure Land.

Because beings in a Buddha's Pure Land can control their death and rebirth, they can take any kind of rebirth they wish in order to benefit others. If they want to take a human rebirth they can do so – they can choose their place of rebirth, parents, family, and so forth according to their karmic connections.

There are many different powa practices, such as those of Amitabha, Tara, Avalokiteshvara, Heruka, and Vajrayogini. The one presented here is the powa of Avalokiteshvara, the Buddha of compassion. This powa has the same function as the powas of Heruka and Vajrayogini because they are all Buddhas of compassion. Our ability to use powa to help the dying and those who have recently died will depend upon the strength of our compassion, and sincere reliance upon Avalokiteshvara is a powerful cause of developing compassion. If we have powerful compassion for all living beings we can definitely help them. Furthermore, extending our compassion to include all living beings is a powerful method for purifying our mind, and if our mind is pure we shall easily attain the Pure Land of a Buddha.

The way to practise the powa of Buddha Avalokiteshvara is explained under the following four headings:

1 Engaging in the preliminary practices
2 Training in the actual powa meditation
3 Applying the practice of powa at the time of death
4 Applying the practice of powa for the benefit of others

ENGAGING IN THE PRELIMINARY PRACTICES

Success in our powa meditation depends upon purifying our negativity, accumulating merit, and receiving the blessings of the Buddhas. We can accomplish these by engaging in the preliminary practices. These have two parts:

1 The practice during the meditation session
2 The practice during the meditation break

THE PRACTICE DURING THE MEDITATION SESSION

We train in the preliminary practices and in the actual powa meditation using the sadhana *Pathway to the Pure Land*, which can be found in Appendix II. According to this sadhana, engaging in the preliminary practices during the meditation session has seven parts:

1 Going for refuge and generating bodhichitta
2 Visualizing Arya Avalokiteshvara
3 Prayer of seven limbs
4 Offering the mandala
5 Requesting the five great meanings
6 Mantra recitation
7 The three recognitions

GOING FOR REFUGE AND GENERATING BODHICHITTA

We begin by imagining ourself surrounded by all living beings of the six realms – the gods, demi-gods, and humans of the three higher realms, and the animals, hungry spirits, and hell beings of the three lower realms. For auspiciousness we visualize them all in human form, but we understand their real nature to be beings of the six realms, each experiencing their own particular form of suffering.

Focusing on all these beings we think:

These countless beings, who are all my mothers, have to experience the suffering of uncontrolled death and rebirth again and again, in life after life. How wonderful it would be if they were to attain permanent liberation from this suffering. May they attain liberation.

Having generated this feeling of compassion from the depths of our heart, we meditate on it for as long as possible. This is a powerful method for purifying our mind.

We then contemplate:

Permanent liberation from suffering can be attained only by relying sincerely upon the Three Jewels: the enlightened beings, the Buddha Jewel; the spiritual realizations, the Dharma Jewel; and the Superior Bodhisattvas, the Sangha Jewel. To liberate all mother sentient beings from their suffering I must accomplish the state of the Three Jewels as my ultimate refuge. Through gaining spiritual realizations I shall become a Superior Bodhisattva, and finally an enlightened being.

Keeping this determination firmly in our mind, we recite three times the prayer of going for refuge and generating bodhichitta.

VISUALIZING ARYA AVALOKITESHVARA

We imagine that on our crown, and the crowns of all the living beings around us, the compassion of all Buddhas appears in the aspect of the letter HRIH standing on a white lotus and a moon seat. The letter HRIH transforms into Avalokiteshvara, the manifestation of all enlightened beings.

He has a white-coloured body, the nature of wisdom light, and four hands indicating that he has completed the realizations of the four noble truths. His first two hands in the mudra of prayer hold a jewel at his heart; the jewel symbolizes the precious jewel of enlightenment, and the prayer mudra shows his respect for his Spiritual Guide, Buddha Amitabha, on his crown. His second right hand holds a crystal mala, indicating that he has the ability to release all living beings from samsara, the cycle of uncontrolled death and rebirth; and his second left hand holds a white lotus flower, symbolizing the purity of his body, speech, and mind.

Avalokiteshvara wears precious silk garments and is adorned with breathtaking jewelled ornaments. His crown is adorned with Buddha Amitabha. He sits on a lotus and moon seat, with his legs crossed in the vajra posture. His upper garment of an antelope skin is not a real skin but a manifestation of his compassionate mind, and indicates that his real nature is compassion. We recognize him to be the same mental continuum as our Spiritual Guide and the synthesis of all Buddhas. We meditate on this visualization without distraction.

We also imagine that the whole ground is filled with living beings engaging in the three activities of purifying negativity, accumulating merit, and receiving blessings from the Buddhas; and that the entire space above them is pervaded by enlightened beings bestowing their blessings.

PRAYER OF SEVEN LIMBS

To purify our negative karma, accumulate merit, and receive blessings we now engage in the practice of the seven limbs: prostration, offering, confession, rejoicing, beseeching the holy beings to remain, requesting the turning of the Wheel of Dharma, and dedication.

PROSTRATION

With deep faith in the holy beings in the space above us, we imagine that from every pore of our body we emanate another body, and that from every pore of these bodies we emanate yet more bodies, until our emanated bodies fill the whole world. We strongly believe that all these countless bodies make prostrations to the holy beings, and we concentrate on this for a while.

OFFERING

We recall that not even the smallest atom of form exists from the side of the object, and by concentrating deeply on this we dissolve all appearances of form into emptiness, the ultimate nature of form. In the same way we recall that sounds, smells, tastes, and tactile objects do not exist from their own side, and by concentrating deeply on this we dissolve all appearances of sounds, smells, tastes, and tactile objects into emptiness, their ultimate nature.

We then imagine that the ultimate nature of all forms that exist throughout infinite worlds appears in the aspect of countless Rupavajra Goddesses – female Deities, white in colour, holding mirrors reflecting the whole universe, who are born from omniscient wisdom mixed completely with the ultimate nature of all forms. The whole of space is pervaded by these beautiful goddesses, and we offer them to Avalokiteshvara, the Buddha of compassion.

We then imagine that the ultimate nature of all sounds that exist throughout infinite worlds appears in the aspect of countless Shaptavajra Goddesses – female Deities, blue in colour, holding flutes that spontaneously produce enchanting music, who are born from omniscient wisdom mixed completely with the ultimate nature of all sounds. The whole of space is pervaded by these beautiful goddesses, and we offer them to Avalokiteshvara, the Buddha of compassion.

We then imagine that the ultimate nature of all smells that exist throughout infinite worlds appears in the aspect of countless Gändhavajra Goddesses – female Deities, yellow in colour, holding beautiful jewelled shells filled with special perfumes whose fragrance pervades the whole world, who are born from omniscient wisdom mixed completely with the ultimate nature of all smells. The whole of space is pervaded by these beautiful goddesses, and we offer them to Avalokiteshvara, the Buddha of compassion.

With the same understanding we offer infinite Rasavajra Goddesses – female Deities, red in colour, holding jewelled vessels filled with nectar possessing three qualities – medicine nectar that cures all disease, life nectar that overcomes death, and wisdom nectar that destroys delusions – who are born from omniscient wisdom mixed completely with the ultimate nature of all tastes.

We then offer infinite Parshavajra Goddesses – female Deities, green in colour, holding precious garments that are supremely soft to the touch, who are born from omniscient wisdom mixed completely with the ultimate nature of all tactile objects.

We receive five benefits from making these offerings: (1) we accumulate great merit, (2) we increase our knowledge of the profound view of emptiness, thereby accumulating a great collection of wisdom, (3) we develop and increase great bliss, (4) we purify ordinary appearances and conceptions, and (5) we gain the opportunity to experience the pure environments and enjoyments of a Buddha.

This profound offering practice is the method for purifying our objects of enjoyment, and the mandala offering explained below is the method for purifying our environment. Together these two practices create the cause for us to take rebirth in the Pure Land of a Buddha with a pure body, experiencing pure enjoyments and pure environments.

While we have this precious human life our main objective must be to attain permanent liberation from suffering, nirvana. This can only be achieved by gaining the realizations of the three higher trainings – higher moral discipline, higher concentration, and higher wisdom; but because our delusions are so strong and we have many bad habits we find it difficult to accomplish these realizations. The only other possibility of freeing ourself from samsaric suffering is to take rebirth in the Pure Land of a Buddha through engaging in powa practice.

CONFESSION

Since beginningless time we have created many negativities through our bodily, verbal, and mental actions. If these actions ripen on us they will result in our taking countless rebirths as hell beings, hungry spirits, and animals. Moreover, many times in both this and previous lives we have broken our spiritual commitments and the three sets of vows – the Pratimoksha, Bodhisattva, and Tantric vows. The result of these transgressions is that our spiritual progress will be retarded and we shall find it more difficult to gain realizations. In particular, our negativity is a serious obstacle to rebirth in a Pure Land. Realizing this we generate deep regret and decide very strongly not to repeat such actions in the future. On the basis of this decision we purify our negativities by confessing them to Avalokiteshvara, the Buddha of compassion.

REJOICING

We contemplate:

All these enlightened beings were once the same as I am now, wandering the paths of samsara and experiencing repeated suffering. However, by applying great effort they entered the Bodhisattva's path, progressed through all its stages, and finally attained the Path of No More Learning, the full enlightenment of a Buddha.

Deeply rejoicing in their virtuous attainments, we make a determination to follow their example. We then meditate on this determination.

BESEECHING THE HOLY BEINGS TO REMAIN

We contemplate:

All the Spiritual Guides who lead sentient beings along the path to liberation are manifestations of Avalokiteshvara, the compassion of all Buddhas. If they were no longer to appear in this world we would have no opportunity to go for refuge or to accumulate merit, and there would be no way for us to escape from the sufferings of samsara and gain pure happiness. From a spiritual point of view the world would be plunged into darkness.

To prevent this from happening we now request the holy beings, the Buddhas, to remain for countless aeons as emanations who will lead sentient beings along the spiritual path. This practice is a very powerful method for accumulating merit, and is extremely important for the future happiness of sentient beings.

REQUESTING THE TURNING OF THE WHEEL OF DHARMA

As a result of the gods Brahma and Indra requesting Buddha to turn the Wheel of Dharma, Buddha gave many Dharma teachings, which are the methods for curing the diseases of the delusions. Since that time countless sentient beings have attained complete liberation from samsaric suffering by sincerely practising Buddha's teachings. So that sentient beings will continue to benefit from the presence of Dharma in this world, we too make a special request to the holy beings to teach the precious Dharma.

DEDICATION

There is a prayer that says:

By my riding the horse of virtue,
Directing it along correct paths with the reins of
    dedication,
And urging it with the whip of joyous effort,
May all beings reach the city of great liberation.

Since the attainment of great liberation, or enlightenment, depends upon pure Buddhadharma flourishing, we dedicate all our virtues to this end and pray that all sentient beings will thereby attain great enlightenment. In particular, we dedicate all our virtuous actions to completing the profound path of transference of consciousness, powa.

OFFERING THE MANDALA

The word 'mandala' in this context means 'universe'. When we offer a mandala to the holy beings we are offering everything – the whole universe with all its objects and all the beings who inhabit it. Since the merit we create when we make an offering accords with the nature of that offering, we mentally transform the whole universe into a Pure Land and imagine that it is filled with precious objects. We then imagine that we are offering this pure universe in our hands.

A child once filled a bowl with dust, and, imagining that the dust was gold, offered it to Buddha Kashyapa. As a result of this pure offering the child was reborn as the wealthy King Ashoka. Likewise, if we offer the world as a Pure Land filled with exquisite objects and precious symbols we shall experience pure environments and pure enjoyments in the future.

REQUESTING THE FIVE GREAT MEANINGS

After offering the prayer of seven limbs and the mandala we request the five great meanings. We ask Arya Avalokiteshvara on our crown to listen to our prayers:

**O Arya Avalokiteshvara, Treasure of Compassion,
And all your retinue, please listen to me.**

Then we request the first great meaning:

**Please quickly release me and all my mothers and
  fathers,
The six classes of living being, from the ocean of
  samsara.**

Visualizing all the living beings around us, who countless times have been our kind mothers and fathers, we develop a mind of great compassion and request Avalokiteshvara to free them all from the sufferings of the six realms. Then we make the second request:

**Please generate quickly in our mental continuum
The vast and profound Dharma of the unsurpassed
    bodhichitta.**

Here 'vast' means the method practices such as compassion and conventional bodhichitta, and 'profound' means the wisdom practices such as the wisdom realizing emptiness and ultimate bodhichitta. To attain enlightenment we need realizations of both method and wisdom, and so we request Avalokiteshvara to bless us to generate these realizations quickly within our mental continuum.

    The third request is:

**With your compassionate nectar please purify
    swiftly
The karma and delusion we have accumulated since
    beginningless time.**

This request is very important. Because since beginningless time we have been accumulating negative karma under the influence of delusions, we are here requesting Avalokiteshvara to bless us so that we may swiftly purify our minds and become free from negative karma, without which there is no possibility of our completing the spiritual path and attaining full enlightenment.

    The fourth request is:

**And with your hands of compassion please swiftly
    lead me
And all living beings to the Pure Land of Bliss.**

If we practise Dharma sincerely in this life and gain stable realizations, these will act as the supreme powa at the time

Buddha Leader of the Heroes

Buddha Glorious Pleasure   *Buddha Jewel Fire*

of our death and transfer our consciousness to a higher rebirth. However, if we do not gain stable realizations in time, we must rely upon a powa practice to transfer our consciousness to a Buddha's Pure Land, where we can complete our spiritual training unhindered by samsaric sufferings.

With this fourth prayer we are requesting Avalokiteshvara to lead us to the Pure Land. The particular Pure Land in which we shall be reborn as a result of this practice depends upon our karmic connections. Practitioners of Heruka and Vajrayogini will take rebirth in the Pure Land of Heruka and Vajrayogini because they have a special connection with these enlightened beings, whereas practitioners of Avalokiteshvara or Amitabha will be reborn in the Pure Land of Bliss, and so on.

Finally we make the fifth request:

O Amitabha and Avalokiteshvara,
Throughout all our lives please be our Spiritual
 Guide;
And by perfectly revealing the unmistaken path
Please lead us all swiftly to the state of
 Buddhahood.

Here we are praying that in all our future lives we shall meet a Spiritual Guide who is an emanation of Amitabha and Avalokiteshvara so that we can continue to practise the stages of the path to enlightenment until we eventually become a fully enlightened Buddha.

It is important to make these requests with strong faith. If we do so repeatedly it is definitely possible that one day we shall see Avalokiteshvara directly. The Indian Buddhist Master Chandrakirti used to study at the great Buddhist monastery of Nalanda, where he would often debate with a scholar called Chandragomin. Chandrakirti was a monk, and Chandragomin a lay practitioner. Both were very famous scholars with many followers, but from a conventional point of view they held different views; Chandrakirti held the

Madhyamika-Prasangika view, and Chandragomin the Chittamatrin view. They would debate these views for days at a time. There were no politics involved – they were simply trying to determine who was correct and who was incorrect.

Chandragomin often found himself close to being defeated by Chandrakirti because he found it difficult to give answers to Chandrakirti's penetrating questions; and whenever this happened he would ask Chandrakirti if he could reply the following day. He would then retire to his room and speak directly to Avalokiteshvara, who would give him the correct answers. Chandrakirti assumed that Chandragomin was consulting other Chittamatrin Teachers and had no idea that he was receiving help directly from Avalokiteshvara. Then one day Chandrakirti asked an especially difficult question, which Chandragomin could not answer. As usual Chandragomin said 'I will give you the answer tomorrow'; but this time Chandrakirti asked him 'How will you be able to answer tomorrow what you cannot answer today?' To this Chandragomin replied 'I will ask Avalokiteshvara, and tomorrow I will give you the answer. If I cannot answer tomorrow, you will win the debate.'

That night Chandrakirti stole up to Chandragomin's room and peeped through the window. To his amazement he saw Chandragomin talking directly to Avalokiteshvara! Chandragomin was asking questions, and Avalokiteshvara was patiently giving him the answers. Filled with awe, Chandrakirti immediately developed a wish to meet Avalokiteshvara directly. He rushed into Chandragomin's room, but as soon as he entered, the Deity vanished.

Until then Chandrakirti had regarded Chandragomin as an inferior practitioner, but now he realized that he was very pure, and felt ashamed for having held such a low opinion of him. He returned to his room and did extensive purification. Longing to meet Avalokiteshvara directly as Chandragomin had done, he practised the sadhana of Buddha Avalokiteshvara again and again for many days. After a while he started to have visions of Avalokiteshvara in his dreams and, encouraged by this, he practised even more earnestly, making heartfelt requests to Avalokiteshvara to appear directly to him.

Then one day Avalokiteshvara manifested in front of him. Chandrakirti was delighted, and said to Avalokiteshvara, 'Now I can really benefit others! Please sit on my shoulders so I can show you to everyone else in the town.' Avalokiteshvara replied that even though Chandrakirti was able to see him, others were not. Chandrakirti, however, continued to make strong requests until Avalokiteshvara eventually agreed. Taking Avalokiteshvara on his shoulders Chandrakirti ran through the town, shouting to everyone to come and see his Spiritual Guide and make prostrations to him. Everyone thought he was crazy. No one saw a thing, except for one person with heavy karmic obscurations who saw Chandrakirti with a dead dog on his shoulders, and a woman wine-seller who saw Avalokiteshvara's right foot. Even so, as a result of this slight vision the woman immediately gained a realization of higher concentration and a very peaceful mind. This shows the power of receiving the blessings of holy beings such as Avalokiteshvara.

If we see enlightened beings such as Avalokiteshvara, Manjushri, Tara, Buddha Shakyamuni, or Je Tsongkhapa, this indicates that our mind is becoming pure and that we are becoming a pure being. Such purity of mind comes from relying sincerely upon these holy beings and receiving their blessings. There are many other stories of faithful practitioners receiving a direct vision of Avalokiteshvara; for example, the fully ordained nun Bhikkshuni Palmo received a direct vision of Avalokiteshvara while she was making mandala offerings.

If we rely sincerely upon a Spiritual Guide who is an emanation of Buddha Avalokiteshvara we can eventually become fully enlightened ourself. Enlightenment is not something that is very far away. We all have Buddha nature, and although at the moment it is covered by karmic obstructions, through practising Dharma sincerely we can remove these obstructions and attain the fully enlightened state of a Buddha.

The attainment of Buddhahood comes from inside; our subtle mind becomes a Buddha's mind, and our subtle body becomes a Buddha's body. We do not need to search outside ourself for Buddhahood.

MANTRA RECITATION

As a result of our sincere requests we imagine that from the bodies of all the enlightened beings in the aspect of Avalokiteshvara on our crown, rays of six-coloured lights radiate: white, green, yellow, red, blue, and dark blue. These lights are manifestations of Buddhas Vairochana, Amoghasiddhi, Ratnasambhava, Amitabha, Akshobya, and Vajradhara respectively.

The light rays reach the bodies and minds of all living beings in the six realms, including our own. Our ordinary appearances and mistaken conceptions are completely purified, and our world – the six realms of samsara – is transformed into Avalokiteshvara's Pure Land. Our body, speech, and mind are transformed into the body, speech, and mind of Avalokiteshvara. We now believe that everything – our environment, enjoyments, body, and mind – is completely pure, and we meditate on this pure appearance without distraction. This is a supreme purification practice, and the basis for mantra recitation.

We then generate a special recognition that whatever appears to us, whatever we hear, and whatever we conceive is inseparable from the Dharmakaya; nothing exists separate from the Dharmakaya. While holding this recognition we recite the mantra of Avalokiteshvara, OM MANI PÄME HUM, to receive powerful blessings from all the enlightened beings. The Dharmakaya is the inner Pure Land of Buddha, so if we maintain this special recognition at the time of our death we shall definitely be reborn in the Pure Land of a Buddha. The definition of Dharmakaya is the union of bliss and emptiness that is complete purity. 'Complete purity' is that which is completely free from the two obstructions – the obstructions to liberation and the obstructions to omniscience.

The mantra has six letters, which are manifestations of the six Buddha families of Vairochana, Amoghasiddhi, Ratnasambhava, Amitabha, Akshobya, and Vajradhara. It has a special power to purify the six delusions of ignorance, attachment, hatred, pride, jealousy, and miserliness, as well as to purify all living beings of the six realms and lead them to the attainment of the six Buddha families. Reciting this mantra with the special recognition explained above purifies our ordinary appearances and conceptions, and through this we shall attain the good fortune to enjoy a Pure Land, a pure body, and a pure mind.

The letter OM symbolizes Avalokiteshvara's body, speech, and mind, and when we recite it we are calling Avalokiteshvara. 'MANI' literally means 'jewel', and in this context refers to enlightenment; and 'PÄME' means 'lotus', and here refers to complete purity. HUM is a request for attainments. Thus, the mantra is a request to Avalokiteshvara to bestow the attainment of complete purity, enlightenment.

THE THREE RECOGNITIONS

To prevent ordinary appearances and conceptions, which are the root of samsara, after the mantra recitation we need continually to maintain the following three recognitions: (1) all the physical forms of ourself and others are manifestations of Arya Avalokiteshvara's body, (2) all sounds are manifestations of the six-letter mantra, and (3) all mental activity arises from great exalted wisdom.

When we are emphasizing the preliminary practices on their own we conclude the session with the following dedication:

By this virtue may I quickly
Become the Buddha of Compassion,
And then lead every living being
Without exception to that ground.

May the precious, supreme bodhichitta
Grow where it has not yet grown;
Where it has grown may it not decrease,
But flourish for evermore.

THE PRACTICE DURING THE MEDITATION BREAK

The time we spend out of meditation is known as the 'meditation break'. Since we spend most of our time out of meditation it is very important to use this time meaningfully.

During our meditation sessions we may experience peaceful states of mind, develop good intentions, and make virtuous determinations; but if we forget these as soon as our session has finished we shall find it impossible to solve our daily problems of anger, attachment, and ignorance, or to make progress in our spiritual practice. We need to maintain the peaceful state of mind we developed during our meditation session continually throughout the day and the night, and to do this we must learn how to integrate our spiritual practice into our daily activities. During the meditation break we should therefore try to accumulate merit, purify our faults and non-virtues, and receive the blessings of the enlightened beings. We should also practise giving, moral discipline, patience, joyous effort, concentration, and wisdom.

To practise giving we can make offerings such as pure water, flowers, incense, lights, perfume, food, and music in front of images of Buddhas, regarding them as actual living Buddhas. We can also give money or other material assistance to the poor and needy, or at the very least we should give food to animals, birds, and insects. We should try to give affectionate love to everyone we meet without exception. We can also give fearlessness by rescuing those who are in danger, and by helping others to overcome their fear, worry, or unhappiness. We can give Dharma teachings and good advice, and dedicate our virtuous actions for the benefit of others.

We should always keep pure moral discipline by avoiding inappropriate actions such as killing, harming others, taking intoxicants, or breaking our spiritual commitments. We should try to act virtuously in everything we think, say, and do, taking every opportunity to act in ways that benefit others.

In these degenerate times the most important practice for us is patience. Impatience gives rise to many of our human problems and is a serious obstacle to our spiritual practice; but if we can sincerely practise patience there will be no basis for us to experience problems, suffering, or obstacles. If someone interferes with the fulfilment of our wishes, or if they harm us either physically or verbally, we should never allow ourself to become angry, recognizing that anger itself is our real enemy. In this way we can continually maintain a peaceful state of mind.

If we are ill or poor, the victim of a natural disaster, separated from those we love, or experiencing other difficult conditions, we should temporarily accept these adversities, happily regarding them as supreme purification. We should strongly pray:

Through my virtue of voluntarily enduring my suffering may all living beings attain permanent liberation from their suffering.

Dedicating our virtue of patience in this way will prevent us from becoming discouraged and unhappy, and will enable us to keep a peaceful mind, no matter what problems may befall us.

To avoid wasting our precious human life we should abandon laziness and put great effort into studying and practising the holy Dharma of Buddha's teachings, which reveal all the stages to the ultimate attainment of full enlighten-ment. In this way we can progress along the spiritual path. If we are lazy we cannot accomplish anything, but if we apply great effort we can accomplish even the highest attain-ment of enlightenment in this short life.

We should not allow ourself to become distracted, engage in meaningless activities, or develop selfish intentions, but instead concentrate on cherishing others. We can transform all our daily activities into the spiritual path simply by changing our intention or motivation.

Finally, we should know through our own experience the meaning of the emptiness of persons and the emptiness of phenomena. By studying authentic teachings and putting them into practice we can improve our wisdom. We shall understand the ultimate nature of all phenomena and how things exist, as well as how to cultivate compassion, bodhi-chitta, and so forth.

If we combine all our daily activities with the six prac-tices of giving, moral discipline, patience, joyous effort, concentration, and wisdom, we shall constantly be accumu-lating merit, purifying negativity, and receiving the bless-ings of the holy beings. These are the supreme conditions for attaining our final goal.

Training in Powa Meditation

As with the preliminary practices, we train in the actual powa meditation using the sadhana *Pathway to the Pure Land*. In each session we begin by engaging in the preliminaries from going for refuge up to the end of the three recognitions as explained in the previous chapter. We then proceed to train in the actual powa meditation. This has six stages:

1 Visualization
2 The three awarenesses
3 Short mandala offering
4 Requests
5 The actual meditation
6 Dedication

VISUALIZATION

We visualize our body in the nature of light, translucent like a rainbow. On the crown of our head is Avalokiteshvara, who is the same mental continuum as our Spiritual Guide and the synthesis of all Buddhas. At Guru Avalokiteshvara's heart the Dharmakaya of all Buddhas appears in the form of an oval-shaped jewel of white light, the size of a thumb. This is Avalokiteshvara's mind and the inner Pure Land of Buddha. We meditate on this visualization for a while.

Then, in the centre of our body, midway between the shoulders but closer to the back than the front, we visualize our central channel. It is translucent, the nature of red light, and the width of an arrow. It begins four finger-widths

Buddha Jewel Moonlight

Buddha Meaningful to Behold   *Buddha Jewel Moon*

below our navel and ascends through the middle of our body to our crown. It is soft and pliant, and very straight. Its lower tip is thin and solid, like the tail of a snake, but as it ascends it becomes wider and hollow. At our crown its upper tip joins the lower door of Avalokiteshvara.

Inside the central channel at our heart we visualize our mind in the form of a sparkling white drop of light with a reddish tint, about the size of a pea.

We now mentally analyze all the aspects of this visualization and try to perceive them clearly. We start with our body of light, then check our central channel, our mind drop, Guru Avalokiteshvara on the crown of our head, and at his heart the Dharmakaya of all Buddhas in the form of the oval-shaped jewel of white light. We then check in reverse order, from the oval-shaped jewel of light at Guru Avalokiteshvara's heart to our body of light. We repeat this checking meditation in serial and reverse orders until we perceive a generic image of the entire visualization, and we then meditate on this without distraction.

After meditating for a while on the complete generic image we concentrate principally on our mind drop. We perceive it clearly and develop the thought, 'I'. In this way we change the basis for imputing our I. Previously the basis for imputing our I was our gross mind and body; now the new basis for imputing our I is our subtle mind and body in the aspect of the drop inside the central channel at our heart.

Our mind drop now strongly thinks:

I must attain permanent liberation from suffering by attaining the Pure Land of a Buddha. I can accomplish this by mixing my mind with the Dharmakaya of all Buddhas, which is the real Pure Land of Buddha.

THE THREE AWARENESSES

We then develop the following three awarenesses:

My mind, the drop, is a traveller going to the Pure Land;
My central channel is the pathway;
The Dharmakaya of all Buddhas at Avalokiteshvara's heart is my destination.

SHORT MANDALA OFFERING

With these special awarenesses we make a short mandala offering to Avalokiteshvara on our crown, recognizing that he is the synthesis of all Buddhas and the same nature as our Spiritual Guide.

REQUESTS

We then make the following requests from the depths of our heart:

O Guru Avalokiteshvara, synthesis of all direct and lineage Gurus,
I request you to dispel all my outer and inner obstacles.
Please bless me to complete the profound path of transference,
And lead me to the supreme Pure Land of Buddha.

O Guru Avalokiteshvara, synthesis of all Deities,
I request you to dispel all my outer and inner obstacles.
Please bless me to complete the profound path of transference,
And lead me to the supreme Pure Land of Buddha.

O Guru Avalokiteshvara, synthesis of all Buddha
  Jewels,
I request you to dispel all my outer and inner
  obstacles.
Please bless me to complete the profound path of
  transference,
And lead me to the supreme Pure Land of Buddha.

O Guru Avalokiteshvara, synthesis of all Dharma
  Jewels,
I request you to dispel all my outer and inner
  obstacles.
Please bless me to complete the profound path of
  transference,
And lead me to the supreme Pure Land of Buddha.

O Guru Avalokiteshvara, synthesis of all Sangha
  Jewels,
I request you to dispel all my outer and inner
  obstacles.
Please bless me to complete the profound path of
  transference,
And lead me to the supreme Pure Land of Buddha.

O Guru Avalokiteshvara, synthesis of all objects of
  refuge,
I request you to dispel all my outer and inner
  obstacles.
Please bless me to complete the profound path of
  transference,
And lead me to the supreme Pure Land of Buddha.

THE ACTUAL MEDITATION

We imagine that as a result of our single-pointed requests,
from the oval-shaped jewel of white light – the Dharmakaya of all Buddhas at Avalokiteshvara's heart – a hook of
white light descends through our central channel and reaches

the mind drop at our heart. As it hooks our drop we draw our downward-voiding wind upwards by making the sound 'HIC' three times, which functions to push our mind drop upwards.

When we make the first HIC, from deep inside our body below the navel, we imagine that our mind drop at the heart chakra is poised to ascend, like a bird about to fly. At the same time our body up to the level of our heart dissolves into the drop.

We then make the second HIC from deep inside our body at our heart. We imagine that our mind drop ascends to the centre of our throat chakra, while at the same time our body up to the level of our throat dissolves into the drop.

We then make the third HIC from the centre of our throat, and imagine that our mind drop ascends to the centre of our crown chakra, while at the same time the rest of our body dissolves into the drop. Our mind drop instantaneously enters the lower door of Avalokiteshvara and, reaching his heart, dissolves inseparably into the Dharmakaya of all Buddhas. We experience the union of bliss and emptiness that is complete purity, and feel that we have reached the Pure Land of Buddha. We remain with this experience single-pointedly for as long as possible.

When we rise from this concentration we imagine that our body, central channel, mind drop, and Avalokiteshvara on our crown appear exactly as before, and we think that we have temporarily returned to this world. Then again our mind drop at our heart develops the wish to go to the Pure Land of Buddha. Mentally we request Avalokiteshvara, 'Please lead me to the supreme Pure Land of Buddha', and then we repeat the above meditation, beginning with the words in the sadhana: 'My body of light is translucent like a rainbow . . . '. In this way we complete the second round of meditation.

We can complete three or seven rounds of this meditation in one session. The third, fourth, fifth, sixth, and seventh rounds are exactly the same as the second, except that in the later rounds the duration of the final meditation on the union of bliss and emptiness should be longer.

DEDICATION

We conclude each session by dedicating all our past, present, and future virtues to our perfecting the practice of powa and thereby attaining great enlightenment.

We need to train in this meditation continually until we are completely familiar with it, at which point we shall be able to apply it when we go to sleep and, finally, at the time of our death. As a result we shall be able to control our death and rebirth and face death with a completely happy and peaceful mind, like a person going on a special holiday. In our next life we shall definitely be reborn in a Buddha Land, such as Sukhavati, Potala, Tushita, Keajra, or any of the twenty-four holy places of Heruka. Alternatively we may choose to be reborn as a human being to whom all environments, enjoyments, bodies, and minds appear as pure. Such a person experiences no samsaric problems. No matter how others may see the world, to him it is pure because his mind is pure. If the mind is pure, the objects appearing to that mind are also pure because objects do not exist from their own side.

As mentioned previously, in general powa involves the mind leaving the body and going to a higher state through the force of meditation. Thus when we are training in powa we are learning to separate our mind from our body through meditation. Although it is sometimes said that successful powa training will gradually shorten one's life span, the training presented here poses no such danger.

This special powa practice has the same function as Vajrayogini's uncommon yoga of inconceivability; through this training we can attain a Buddha's Pure Land such as Pure Dakini Land without abandoning this human body.

This particular instruction is a combination of the common powa instructions, such as those written by the first Panchen Lama and Ngulchu Dharmabhadra, and the uncommon powa instructions that come from the Ganden oral lineage. We are extremely fortunate to have the opportunity to receive and practise this profound instruction.

Practising Powa at the Time of Death

Applying the practice of powa at the time of death has six parts:

1 The causes of death
2 The conditions of death
3 The signs of death
4 The minds of death
5 The sign that dying has ended
6 How to apply the practice of powa at the time of death

THE CAUSES OF DEATH

There are three principal causes of death: the ending of the karmically determined life span, exhaustion of merit, and loss of power of the life force. As a result of having kept moral discipline in a previous life and having engaged in other virtuous actions such as saving others' lives, we have now obtained a human rebirth with the average life span of, say, seventy years. Although we have created the cause for a life of this length it is possible to die earlier or to live longer. Severe negative actions done in this life can shorten our life span, while virtuous actions such as refraining from killing, and caring for the sick, can lengthen it.

Some people die due to lack of merit even though their life span has not ended. They are unable to find the necessities to sustain life, such as food or the right medicine. The few remaining years of their life are then 'carried over' into a future human rebirth, which will probably be short and

Buddha Stainless One

Buddha Bestower of Glory   *Buddha Pure One*

characterized by misfortune. Other people rich in merit can find excellent conditions and thereby manage to live a few years longer than their karmically determined life span.

The third cause of death is loss of power of the life force. The life force is the power of our life-supporting wind. This inner wind, which abides at our heart, functions to maintain the connection between our mind and body. When its strength diminishes, the connection is broken and we die. Illness, spirits, accidents, or a negative and unhealthy life style can all weaken our life force.

If our life span, merit, and life force are all exhausted we shall definitely die, but if one or two of these causes of life remain it is possible to renew the others. For example, if our life span and life force are still intact but our merit has run out, we can create more merit by performing virtuous actions. If our life force is damaged, then, provided we have merit or life span, we can restore it by engaging in practices such as vase breathing at our heart. This is one of the best methods to increase the power of our life-supporting wind. To do this we gather the inner winds from the upper and lower parts of our body at our heart, imagining that they dissolve into our life-supporting wind. Then we hold our winds and mind at the heart, remaining concentrated there for as long as we can.

Our life force is our most precious possession and so we need to stabilize and increase it. Once it is destroyed the damage cannot be repaired. If we lose any other possession our loss can be restored, but once our life span finishes we cannot borrow any more time to complete the tasks of this life. Therefore, if we are wasting our vitality in meaningless pursuits we should feel this as the greatest loss. If our life is short or we squander it we cannot complete our spiritual practice.

THE CONDITIONS OF DEATH

The conditions of death are countless. Some people die of physical illness and others are killed in accidents or natural disasters. Some people are killed by their enemies and others kill themselves. Some people die of starvation, while others die of the food they eat. Although food is one of the most enjoyable things in life, eating unhealthy food is a condition for diseases and degenerative illnesses such as cancer. Anything can become a condition of our death, even the things we consider life-sustaining.

THE SIGNS OF DEATH

The signs of death are of two kinds: distant and close. The distant signs can be experienced even when we are not suffering from any particular illness. They are experienced between six and three months before we die, and are of three kinds: bodily signs, mental signs, and dream signs. They do not necessarily indicate that we shall soon die, but if they persist this means that death is probably imminent. If we know what these distant signs of death are, we shall know when we are experiencing them, and so we shall be warned to make preparations that will benefit our future life. We shall know that it is time to make sure that we are engaging in pure Dharma practice and to apply any methods we have learnt for extending our life span, such as the practices of Amitayus and White Tara. If these are not successful we should definitely apply the practice of powa.

Some of the distant bodily signs of death are the following: while we are passing urine or excrement we continuously hiccup; we can no longer hear the buzzing sound of our inner ear when we block our ears; when we apply pressure against our fingernails and then release it the blood does not quickly return; during sexual intercourse, if we are a woman we release white drops instead of red and if we are a man we release red drops instead of white;

for no reason we cannot taste things; for no reason we cannot smell things; our exhaled breath is cold – when we blow on our hand it feels cold instead of warm; our tongue shrinks and feels rolled or swollen, and when we poke it out we can no longer see its tip; in the dark when we press the top of our eyeball with our finger so that the eyeball protrudes a little we can no longer see colourful shapes and patterns; we hallucinate a sun at night; when we sit in the sun in the morning we can no longer see in our shadow streams of energy flowing from the crown of our head; saliva no longer forms in our mouth; the end of our nose becomes pinched; black marks appear on our teeth; our eyeballs sink further into the hollows of our eyes.

Distant mental signs of death include: a change in our usual temperament – for example, we become aggressive when we are usually kind and gentle, or we become gentle when we are usually aggressive and ill-tempered; for no reason we begin to dislike the place where we live, our friends, or other objects of attachment; we feel sad for no reason; our wisdom and intelligence become less clear and less powerful.

Distant dream signs include repeated dreams that we are falling from a high mountain, that we are naked, or that we are travelling south on our own across a desert.

The close signs of death will be explained later.

THE MINDS OF DEATH

The minds we have when we are dying are of two types, gross and subtle. Whereas the gross minds of death can be virtuous, non-virtuous, or neutral, for ordinary beings the subtle minds of death are only neutral. When we are dying, if our last gross mind is virtuous it will cause the good potentialities carried in our mind to ripen as a virtuous mental action that will lead us directly to higher rebirth as a human or a god. A virtuous mind at death is like water – it nourishes the virtuous potentialities that remain like dry seeds within our field-like consciousness. If two kinds of seed, barley seeds and wheat seeds, are sown in a field, but only the wheat seeds are watered, these will be certain to ripen first. In a similar way, while we still carry both virtuous and non-virtuous potentialities within our mind, a virtuous mind at the time of death will ensure that our virtuous potentialities are the ones that will ripen. This holds even if we have led an immoral life and committed many non-virtuous actions. However, we do not thereby escape the effects of all our non-virtuous deeds. If we take a human rebirth our life may be afflicted with great suffering or our life span may be short. If we do not purify our negative karma we shall eventually experience the fully ripened effect of our actions by taking rebirth in the lower realms.

Sometimes people who have no interest in spiritual practice and who lead careless, immoral lives enjoy better conditions and greater worldly success than people who are practising Dharma. Observing this, we may sometimes feel discouraged and think 'What is the point of practising Dharma?! Other people are not even trying to lead good lives but good things just fall into their laps, whereas although I practise diligently I seem to experience only hardship for all my pains.' If we start to think like this it is because we are viewing only the present situation and have not fully understood how actions and their effects follow in succession. If we are now experiencing difficulties, these are the effects of our past actions. They are not the effects of our present spiritual practice, for the effects of our present spiritual practice will be happiness in the future. In the same way, the good fortune of people who are not interested in spiritual practice is the effect of merit they created in the past and is not a result of their present life style. Whatever harmful actions they commit in this life will bring hardships in the future.

When we die, if our last gross mind is non-virtuous it will cause the bad potentialities we carry in our mind to ripen as a non-virtuous mental action, and this will lead us directly to a lower rebirth. From this we can see how important it is to develop a happy and virtuous state of mind at the time of death. We can also see how we can be of great benefit to others when they are dying, by encouraging them to develop a positive mind and creating for them conditions that will help them to generate good thoughts. In this way we can bring measureless benefit to our friends and relatives, even if they have no interest in Dharma. One of the greatest acts of kindness that we can show someone else is to help them to die peacefully and with a virtuous mind, for if in this way they attain a happy rebirth they will have attained the same result as someone who has successfully practised powa.

When the gross minds of death have ceased and the mind becomes the subtle mind of death, there are no gross feelings – pleasant, painful, or neutral – and no gross discriminations. Since for ordinary beings the subtle minds of death are neutral, these are powerless to induce virtuous minds.

THE SIGN THAT DYING HAS ENDED

When we have experienced the distant signs of death, the close signs of death will occur. First the earth element of the body dissolves. The external sign of this dissolution is that the body becomes thin; and the internal sign is a mirage-like appearance to the mind. Next, the water element dissolves. The external sign is that the mouth and tongue become very dry, and the liquids of the body, such as urine, blood, and sperm, decrease; and the internal sign is a smoke-like appearance to the mind. Next the fire element dissolves. The external sign of this dissolution is reduced warmth of the body and coldness in the area around the navel, the centre of the body's heat; and the internal sign is a sparkling-fireflies-like appearance. Next the wind element dissolves. The external sign is reduced power of movement due to the decreasing power of the winds that flow through the channels of the body and cause us to generate gross minds; and the internal sign is a candle-flame-like appearance. The mind perceiving this appearance is the last gross mind of death.

The first subtle mind of death is the mind perceiving a white appearance. When this appearance ceases, the mind has become more subtle and perceives a red appearance. This mind again becomes more subtle and transforms into the mind of black near-attainment, to which only black appears. At this stage it is as if the dying person has no memory. Since there is no physical movement, no heart-beat, and no movement in the channels, some people think that this is the end of dying; but in fact the consciousness has not yet left the body. The mind of black near-attainment transforms into the most subtle mind perceiving the clear light of death, a clear bright appearance like the light of dawn. This is the sign that the most subtle mind that resides within the indestructible drop at the heart has manifested and all other minds have ceased to manifest. Then the indestructible drop opens, and its white and red parts separate, releasing the consciousness, which immediately departs from the body. The white drop descends through the central channel to emerge through the tip of the sex organ, and the red drop ascends through the central channel to emerge through the nostrils. When this happens it is the sign that the consciousness has left the body and the process of dying has ended.

HOW TO APPLY THE PRACTICE OF POWA
AT THE TIME OF DEATH

Having become familiar with the practice of powa, when we perceive the distant signs of death, or understand that we do not have very long to live, we need to practise both the preliminaries and the actual meditation day and night.

We should abandon attachment for our families, friends, and possessions – indeed for all the things of this life. A person who stays in a luxury hotel for a few days has no attachment to the hotel because he knows that he will soon have to leave. In the same way there is no sense in developing attachment to the things of this life because we know that we shall soon have to leave everything behind.

We should encourage ourself by thinking:

Now is the time to go the Pure Land of Buddha, where all my samsaric problems will come to an end and I shall enjoy pure environments, pure enjoyments, a pure body, and a pure mind. My life in the Pure Land will be superior in every respect to my present life. How fortunate I am!

Thinking like this we should follow the example of Long-döl Lama and make a strong determination to go to the Pure Land without any attachment or sense of loss for this life. With this determination we should engage in powa practice continually.

As soon as we experience the close signs of death it is of utmost importance that we concentrate mainly on the feeling that our mind is mixed with the Dharmakaya of all Buddhas, the inner Pure Land. We should maintain this feeling with strong mindfulness until our gross minds cease. This is the final station on the way to our destination, the Pure Land of a Buddha.

We should not allow our physical illness or discomfort to interfere with our concentration. We should stop thinking that we are ill, but instead think 'My body is not me, so there is no sense in thinking "I am ill" or "I am in pain"'; and concentrate on the feeling that our mind is mixed with the Dharmakaya. We should die with this feeling.

Buddha Transforming with Purity

Buddha Water Deity   *Buddha God of Water Deities*

Death, Intermediate State, and Rebirth

To appreciate fully the importance of helping those who have died and those who are dying, we first need to understand the process of death, intermediate state, and rebirth. Applying the practice of powa for the benefit of others is therefore presented in two parts:

1 Understanding death, the intermediate state, and rebirth
2 How to apply the practice of powa for the benefit of others

UNDERSTANDING DEATH, THE INTERMEDIATE STATE, AND REBIRTH

This has three parts:

1 Understanding death
2 Understanding the intermediate state
3 Understanding rebirth

UNDERSTANDING DEATH

Death will definitely come and nothing can prevent it. No matter where we are born, whether it be in fortunate or unfortunate states of existence, we shall definitely have to die. Whether we are born in the happiest condition of samsara or in the deepest hell we shall have to experience death. However far and wide we travel we shall never find a place where we can hide from death, even if we voyage far into space or tunnel deep underground.

Although Buddha's Truth Body is deathless, his Emanation Bodies pass away. When Buddha Shakyamuni was
about to pass away, over ten thousand Foe Destroyers
(those who have attained nirvana), including Shariputra,
one of his close disciples, chose to die because they could
not bear the sorrow of having to witness Buddha's death.
Then Buddha asked his disciples to make his last throne in
Kushinagar, where he gave his final teaching: 'All produced phenomena are impermanent.' To those with pure
karma he revealed the signs and indications of a Buddha's
body; and then, remaining on his throne, he demonstrated
how to die. Whether or not Foe Destroyers and the Emanation Bodies of Buddhas remain in this world depends
upon the karma of the beings who live here. When our
good karma and merit decrease, Foe Destroyers and the
emanations of Buddhas become fewer and fewer.

No one alive at the time of Buddha Shakyamuni remains
alive today, and no one alive at the time of Buddha's disciple, Mahakashyapa, remains alive today. Only their names
survive. All those who were alive two hundred years ago
have passed away, and all who live now will be gone in two
hundred years' time. Understanding this we should ask
ourself 'Could I alone outlive death?'

When our ripening karma to experience this life comes
to an end, no one can prevent our death, not even Buddha.
Once in ancient times two Indian clans, the Pakyepas and
the Shakyapas, were waging war against one other. The king
of the Pakyepas resolved to massacre all the Shakyapas, and
so some of the Shakyapas took their children to Buddha
for protection. Shariputra offered to protect all the children
by means of his miracle powers, but with his clairvoyance
Buddha could see that Shariputra would not be able to save
the children because all the Shakyapas had created the
collective karma to die in that war and their karma was
now ripening. However, to console the Shakyapas, Buddha
let Shariputra take the children. Shariputra put some of

them inside Buddha's begging bowl and he hid others in the sun. Nevertheless, on the same day that the Pakyepas killed all the other Shakyapas, the children inside Buddha's begging bowl and in the sun also perished, although there was no one to inflict death upon them.

When the time of our death arrives there is no escape. If it were possible to prevent death by using clairvoyance or miracle powers, those who possessed such powers would have become immortal; but even clairvoyants die. The most powerful monarchs who have ruled in this world have been helpless before the power of death. The king of beasts, the lion, who can kill an elephant, is immediately destroyed when he encounters the Lord of Death. Even millionaires have no way of avoiding death. They cannot distract death with a bribe and buy time, saying 'If you postpone my death I shall give you wealth beyond your wildest dreams.'

Death is relentless and will not be compromised. In *Sutra Addressed to a King* it is said that death is like the collapse of an immense mountain in all four directions. There is no way to hold back its devastation. In this Sutra, Buddha says:

Ageing is like an immovable mountain.
Decay is like an immovable mountain.
Sickness is like an immovable mountain.
Death is like an immovable mountain.

Ageing progresses surreptitiously and undermines our youth, our strength, and our beauty. Although we are hardly aware of the process, it is already underway and cannot be reversed. Sickness destroys the comfort, power, and strength of our body. If doctors help us to overcome our first illness, others take its place until, eventually, our sickness cannot be removed. In the same Sutra, Buddha says:

We cannot escape from sickness and death by running away from them. We cannot placate them with riches or use miracle powers to make them vanish. Every single being in this world must suffer ageing, sickness, and death.

51

In *Guide to the Bodhisattva's Way of Life* Shantideva says:

Remaining neither day nor night,
This life is always slipping away
And never getting any longer.
How could one such as I avoid death?

From the moment of our conception we head inexorably towards death, just like a racehorse galloping towards its finishing post. Even racehorses occasionally relax their pace, but in our race towards death we never stop, not even for a second. While we are sleeping and while we are awake our life slips away. Every vehicle stops and breaks its journey from time to time, but our life span never stops running out. One moment after our birth, part of our life span has perished. We live in the very embrace of death. The seventh Dalai Lama said:

After our birth we have no freedom to remain even
for a minute.
We head towards the embrace of the Lord of Death
like an athlete running.
We may think that we are among the living, but our
life is the very highway of death.

Suppose our doctor were to break the news to us that we are suffering from an incurable disease and that we have only one week left to live. If our friend were then to offer us a fantastic gift such as a diamond, a new car, or a free holiday we would not get very excited about it. Yet in reality this is our very predicament, for we are all suffering from a mortal disease. How foolish it is to become overly interested in the passing pleasures of this brief life!

If we find it difficult to think about our approaching death we can just listen to a clock ticking and be aware that every tick marks the end of a moment of our life and draws us closer to death. Atisha used to practise this in his meditations, taking the sound of drops of water as his example.

Or we can imagine that the Lord of Death lives a few miles up the road from our home, and as we listen to the clock ticking we can imagine ourself taking steps in death's direction. In this way we shall become real travellers.

In *Extensive Enjoyment Sutra* Buddha says:

> These three worlds are as impermanent as autumn clouds.
> The birth and death of beings are like the entrance and exit of actors on the stage.

Actors frequently change their costumes and their roles, making their entrance in many different disguises. In the same way, living beings take different forms continually and enter new worlds. Sometimes they are human beings, sometimes they are animals, and sometimes they enter hell. The Sutra continues:

> The life span of a living being passes like lightning in the sky and perishes as quickly as water falling from a high mountain.

Death will come regardless of whether or not we have made the time for spiritual practice. Although life is short, it would not be so bad if we had plenty of time for Dharma practice, but most of our time is taken up with sleeping, working, eating, shopping, talking, and so on, leaving very little time for pure practice. Our whole time is easily consumed by other pursuits until, suddenly, we die.

We keep thinking that we have plenty of time for our spiritual practice, but if we closely examine our way of life we shall see that the days slip by without our getting down to serious practice. If we do not make the time to engage in Dharma purely, at the time of death we shall be like Mondrol Chödak; we shall look back on our life and see that it has been of very little benefit. However, if we are continually aware of our death we shall develop such a sincere wish to practise purely that we shall naturally begin to modify our daily routine so that it includes at least a little time for spiritual practice, until eventually we shall find more time for practice than for other things.

Thinking about our impending death again and again we may feel afraid; but it is not enough just to feel fear. Once we have generated an appropriate fear of dying unprepared we should search for something that will offer real protection. Gungtang Jampelyang said that the paths of future lives are very long and unfamiliar. We have to experience life after life and we cannot be sure where we shall take rebirth – whether we shall have to follow the path to unhappy states of existence or the paths to happier realms. We have no freedom or independence but must go wherever our karma takes us. Therefore we need to find something that will show us a safe way to future lives, something that will direct us along correct paths and away from wrong paths. We must make effort with our body, speech, and mind to put Dharma into practice. The possessions and enjoyments of samsara cannot help us. Only Dharma reveals a flawless path. Since it is the only possession and enjoyment that will help and protect us in the future, we must make effort with our body, speech, and mind to put it into practice. Milarepa said:

> There are more fears in future lives than in this one.
> Have you prepared anything that will help you? If you
> have not prepared for your future lives, do so now.
> The only protection against those fears is the practice
> of holy Dharma.

If we think about our own life we shall see that we have spent many years with no interest in spiritual practice, and that even now that we have the wish to practise, still, due to laziness, we do not practise purely. Gungtang Jampelyang said:

> I spent twenty years not wanting to practise Dharma.
> I spent the next twenty years thinking that I could

practise later on. I spent another twenty years engrossed in other activities and regretting the fact that I had not engaged in Dharma practice. This is the story of my empty human life.

This could be our own life story, but if we are aware of the inevitability of our death we shall avoid wasting our precious human life and we shall strive to make it meaningful.

Sometimes we fool ourself by thinking 'I am young and so I shall not die soon', but we can see how misguided this thought is merely by observing how many young people die before their parents. Sometimes we think 'I am healthy and so I shall not die soon', but we can see that people who are healthy and looking after the sick sometimes die before their patients. People who go to visit their friends in hospital may die sooner in a car crash, for death does not confine itself to those who are aged and unwell. Someone who is alive and well in the morning could be dead by the afternoon, and someone who is well when he falls asleep may die before he wakes up. Some people die while they are eating and some people die in the middle of a conversation. Some people die as soon as they are born.

Death may not give any warning. This enemy can come at any time and often he strikes quickly, when we least expect it. He may come as we are driving to a party, or switching on our television, or as we are thinking to ourself 'I shall not die today' and making plans for our summer holidays or our retirement. The Lord of Death can creep up on us as dark clouds creep across the sky. Sometimes when we go indoors the sky is bright and clear, but when we step outside again the sky is overcast. In the same way death can quickly cast its shadow across our life.

Although our death is certain and our life span is indefinite it would not be so bad if the conditions that lead to death were rare; but there are innumerable external and internal conditions that can bring about our death. It is said that there are eighty thousand types of obstacle or spirit that can destroy our vitality. All of these are conditions that could bring about our death. The external environment causes death by famine, floods, fires, earthquakes, pollution, and so on. In a similar way, the internal elements of our body cause death when their harmony is lost and one of them develops in excess. When the internal elements are in harmony they are said to be like four snakes of the same species and strength abiding together peacefully; but when they lose their harmony it is like one snake becoming stronger than the others and consuming them, until finally it dies of hunger itself.

Besides these inanimate causes of death, other living beings such as thieves, hostile soldiers, and wild beasts can bring about our death. Even things that we do not consider to be threatening, things that we think of as supporting and protecting our life, such as our house, our car, or our best friend, can turn out to be causes of our death. People are sometimes crushed to death by their own house or they fall to their death from their own staircase, and each day many people are killed in their cars. Some people die on holiday and some people are killed by their own hobbies and entertainments, such as horse riders who are thrown to their death. Even our friends and lovers can become causes of our death, by mistake or by intention. We read in the newspapers how lovers sometimes kill one another and how parents sometimes kill their own children. The very food we eat to nourish and sustain our life can be the cause of death. If we investigate carefully we shall not be able to find any worldly enjoyment that is not a potential cause of death and that is solely a cause of remaining alive. Protector Nagarjuna said:

> We maintain our life in the midst of thousands of conditions that threaten death. Our life force abides like a candle flame in the breeze. The candle flame of our life is easily extinguished by the winds of death that blow from all directions.

Each person has created the karma to remain in this life for a certain period, but since we cannot remember what karma we have created we cannot know the exact duration of our present life. As mentioned earlier, it is possible for us to die an untimely death before completing our life span because we can exhaust our merit sooner than we exhaust the karma that determines our life span. If this happens we become so ill that doctors cannot help us, or we find that we are unable to obtain food and other necessities to support our life. However, even when we become seriously ill, if our life span has not ended and we still have merit we can find all the conditions necessary for recovery.

In *Pile of Jewels Sutra* nine main conditions of untimely death are mentioned:

(1) Eating without moderation.
(2) Eating unwholesome food.
(3) Eating food before having properly digested our previous meal.
(4) Retaining undigested food in our stomach for a long time without eliminating.
(5) Vomiting digested food.
(6) Not taking the right medicine.
(7) Not having appropriate skills – such as trying to swim or drive a car without knowing how to.
(8) Travelling at the wrong time – such as driving through a red traffic light or jogging at noon at the height of summer in a very hot country.
(9) Indulging in sex without restraint.

Although Secret Mantra teaches methods for prolonging our life span, they work only if we practise them purely with strong faith and good concentration, and if our meditation is very powerful. Thus at present it is very difficult to extend our life span.

Although there are many causes of death it would not be so bad if our bodies were strong like steel, but they are delicate. It does not take guns and bombs to destroy them; they can be destroyed by a small needle. In *Friendly Letter* Nagarjuna says:

> There are many destroyers of our life force.
> Our human body is like a water bubble.

Just as a water bubble bursts as soon as it is touched, so a single drop of water in the heart or the slightest scratch from a poisonous thorn can cause our death. In the same text Nagarjuna says that at the end of this aeon the entire world system will be consumed by fire and not even its ashes will remain. Since the entire universe will become empty, there is no need to say that this delicate human body will decay most swiftly.

We can contemplate the process of our breathing and how it continues without break between inhalation and exhalation. If it were to stop, we would die. Yet even when we are asleep and our mindfulness is not functioning, our breathing continues, although in many other respects we resemble a corpse. Nagarjuna said 'This is a most wonderful thing!' When we wake up in the morning we should rejoice, thinking 'How amazing it is that my breathing has sustained my life throughout sleep. If it had ceased during the night I would now be dead!'

Even if we were to possess all the wealth in the world, at the time of our death it would be useless because we would not be able to take any part of it along with us and it would not alleviate the slightest bit of our suffering. There is a saying in Tibetan that when death comes the king who sits on a golden throne and the poor man who goes begging from town to town are both equal. In the Sutra called *Glorious Tree* Buddha says:

> Even if you had enough food stocked up to last you one hundred years, when you die you will have to travel to your next life hungry. Even if you had enough clothes

to last you one hundred years, when death comes you will still have to travel to your next life naked.

In *Guide to the Bodhisattva's Way of Life* Shantideva says:

Because I do not realize that
I must leave everything and depart,
I commit various negative actions
On account of my friends and foes.

There was once a man who was labouring very hard to cut a big round stone and make it square. A passer-by asked him 'Why are you working so hard to make this stone square?', and the man replied 'So I can leave it behind.' We are just like this man because we spend so much time and put so much effort into accumulating wealth only to leave it all behind when we die.

In *Guide to the Bodhisattva's Way of Life* Shantideva says:

When I am seized by the messenger of the Lord of
   Death,
What help will my friends and relatives be?
Only merit can protect me at that time,
But upon that I have never relied.

We came into this world alone and we shall depart alone, and there is no one else who can take on the sufferings of our ageing and sickness and share them with us. Our friends and relatives are all equally powerless to help us at the time of our greatest need, the time of our death. Even if everyone in the world were to become our friend, no one would be able to help us at the time of our death. If they were to hold onto our limbs and clutch our head they would still be unable to hold us back from death. The most powerful people in the world have many security guards surrounding them, but no one can offer real security when the Lord of Death arrives. The great Yogi Mitatso once recited this verse to a king:

Buddha Glorious Excellence

Buddha Glorious Sandalwood   *Buddha Endless Splendour*

It does not matter that you are a king with great
  resources.
When it is time for you to pass on to the next life,
  you will have to go alone and in great fear.
You will have to travel without your possessions
  and wealth, without your queen, your children,
  or your servants.

The first Panchen Lama said:

When death comes it parts us from our friends and
relatives so that we never meet them again. It completely destroys the chance of a reunion. There is nothing more severe than this Lord of Death.

In this life, even if we are separated from our friends and
relatives for a very long time it is still possible to meet them
again; but when death intervenes we are finally separated
from our friends and relatives, and when we meet them
again in future lives we do not recognize them and they do
not recognize us.

At the time of death even our own body is of no use.
From the time of our birth we have cherished and protected
our body as our most precious possession, wrapping it up
when it has been cold, anointing it with soothing cream
when it has been grazed, strongly defending it whenever
anyone has tried to harm it. We have such compassion for
our body that we can hardly bear it to suffer any pain. If it
is thirsty we can hardly endure it, and if it becomes weak
and ill we feel miserable. Most of the harmful actions we
have committed have been done for the sake of our own
body. We carefully tend to all its needs – clothing it, feeding
it, washing it, and enhancing it. If someone insults our
body, saying something like 'Your legs are fat' or 'You look
like a monkey', we cannot stand it; but if someone says the
same things about our friend's body we do not think it
matters and we may even laugh. Yet this body that we
cherish so dearly is treacherous. It deceives us most at the

time of death, when it completely deserts us, even though we urgently need its help. The first Panchen Lama said:

> This body that we have cherished for so long cheats us at the time when we need it most.

Some people think that death is like a candle flame going out, but death cannot be like that. When a candle flame is extinguished its continuum ceases and it completely disappears, but when we die we do not disappear. Our death is like a bird flying from its nest; our body is like the nest and our mind is like the bird. When our consciousness leaves this body we continue to experience fear and hallucinations, we suffer and still need protection. If we practise Dharma we create good habits of mind that continue into our next life. Since the continuum of our consciousness carries the mental habits we have cultivated, our spiritual practice and virtuous actions of this life can help us at the time of our death and in all our future lives.

Sometimes it is very helpful to imagine that the time of our death has come. We know that we shall definitely die, whether through sickness or by accident, and we shall probably die in hospital. When we become ill we shall be taken there and at first our doctor may think that he can cure us. Eventually he will give up hope and stop coming to see us. When our relatives find out that he has given up hope they will feel helpless and distressed, but all they will be able to do is weep. As we begin to die, our body will lose its warmth and we shall start to find it difficult to breathe. Our body will become weak and shrunken and we shall not be able to hear sounds properly or see forms clearly. If our friends and relatives are standing around us we shall not recognize them. Our tongue will become short so that we cannot speak coherently. Gradually our memory will fade, but before it has completely disappeared we shall realize that we are dying and become deeply distressed. We shall think desperately 'How wonderful it would be if I could live longer', and we shall inwardly beg our friends and relatives to help us, but they will be completely powerless. Slowly, as the four internal elements absorb, we shall perceive the different appearances and hallucinations. At times we shall experience fear. Our memory will become more and more subtle until all the appearances of this life have vanished. This will be the end of everything in this life – the end of living in our house, the end of meeting our friends, the end of talking to our family.

If we find it difficult to use our imagination in this way, we can visit cemeteries and look at the gravestones, remembering that underneath each one lies a dead body. We can take one grave as an example. Suppose the inscription reads 'Here lies Peter. Died 21st May, 1999'. The only difference between Peter and us is a small matter of time. In a while we shall go where Peter has gone, and just as his body now lies here rotting in the ground, so this body of ours will soon be buried and decomposing.

Many other things can remind us of death. Every night on television we can watch people die. Usually we watch only to gather information or to be entertained; but if we are interested in gaining a realization of death and impermanence we can identify with the people we see dying and think 'I shall soon become just like that person.' In the same way, when we see old people on television we can think 'I shall soon become just like that person', and when we see sick people we can think 'I shall become like that.' If we practise in this way our television viewing will become very beneficial; some things teach impermanence, some teach emptiness, some teach compassion, and some teach how samsara is in the nature of suffering. With Dharma wisdom we can find a teaching in everything, and all things increase our faith, our wisdom, and our experience of Dharma. Milarepa said he regarded everything that appeared to his mind as a Dharma book. All things confirmed the truth of Buddha's teachings and increased his spiritual experience.

UNDERSTANDING THE INTERMEDIATE STATE

The intermediate state, or bardo, is so called because it is the state between death and the next rebirth. Beings who wander in this state are known as 'bardo beings'. The easiest way to gain conviction of the existence of the bardo is by considering the analogy of the dream state, which closely resembles the bardo. Both the dream body and the bardo body arise in dependence upon subtle energy winds. Both lack flesh, bones, blood, and inner organs, but both have complete sense powers. Just as the dream body develops from the clear light of sleep, so the bardo body develops from the clear light of death; and just as the dream body is known only to the dreamer, so the bardo being is seen only by other bardo beings and not by ordinary beings who do not have eye clairvoyance. The location of the dream body quickly shifts and changes, and acquaintances made in our dream are fleeting. Similarly, the location of the bardo being easily shifts and changes, and acquaintances made in the bardo are short-lived.

As we fall asleep the gross winds gather into our heart and we experience the same signs as the close internal signs of death, from the mirage-like appearance to the clear light. Yogis and some meditators who have developed their mindfulness can be aware of these signs as they fall asleep, but for most people these signs are not clearly perceived because we lack mindfulness during sleep. After the clear light of sleep we do not immediately wake up but we enter the dream state and develop a dream body. In a similar way, as we die, the gross winds gather into our heart and we perceive the internal signs of death. From the clear light of death we do not immediately reawaken into a new life but we enter the bardo and develop a dream-like bardo body.

Bardo beings have five characteristics: (1) they take the shape of their next rebirth – for example, if a human is going to take rebirth as a dog his bardo body will be the shape of a dog, and if a dog is going to take rebirth as a human its bardo body will be the shape of a human; (2) they arise instantaneously with fully formed limbs, sense powers, and so forth; (3) they have contaminated miracle powers – their bodies are not impeded by solid matter so they can, for example, travel through walls and mountains, and they possess contaminated clairvoyance; (4) their vision is not impeded by material things – they can see through physical objects such as houses, and they can see things at a great distance; (5) only bardo beings can perceive other bardo beings – ordinary humans, except some with limited powers of clairvoyance, are unable to see them. Immediately after our death we shall take the form of a bardo being with these five characteristics.

In *Treasury of Abhidharma* by the Buddhist Master Vasubandhu there is a verse that explains the shape of the bardo being. A literal reading of this verse has led some scholars to assert that the shape of a bardo being's body is that of its previous life. This misunderstanding reinforces the false view that bardo beings can recognize and communicate with their former relatives and friends, and that they experience suffering when they are ignored by their former families and friends or when they see them mourning. According to this misunderstanding, when the bardo being sees its relatives eating food, for example, it feels unhappy at not being able to join in; and when it realizes that it has died it experiences intense misery and develops strong aversion towards its former body. However, Vasubandhu, Arya Asanga, and many other scholars taught that the shape of the bardo being is the shape of its future life, not its previous life. Support for this view can be found in Buddha's Sutras. Bardo beings do not recognize anyone or anything from their previous life, including the body they have just left.

Some scholars assert that the life span of a bardo being is seven days. They say that for the first three and a half days the bardo being takes the shape of the body of its previous life, and for the next three and a half days it takes the shape of the body of its future life. Again, the writings of Vasubandhu and Asanga refute this view.

In some popular Tibetan texts there are stories describing the experiences of so-called 'returners from death' – humans who return from the dead, re-animate their corpses, and bring messages to beings in this world from beings in other worlds. Some Sutras, such as the *Medicine Guru Sutra*, when taken literally also seem to imply that the departed consciousness of a dead person can return to its former body. Other texts, such as Dharmakirti's *Commentary to Valid Cognition*, refute this. Which explanation is correct? In reality, the 'returners from death' never really died. To an ordinary observer they were dead – their bodies were cold and they had stopped breathing – but because their subtle consciousness was still inside their body they did not actually die. Once they recovered they remembered everything that had occurred during the 'death process', and they told others about their experiences. It is not possible for someone who has actually died to return to his or her body, because death is the irreversible separation of body and mind.

Beings in the bardo experience many hallucinations. Each bardo being has the karma to experience the particular fears related to their rebirth in a particular realm, especially the three lower realms, but there are three types of terrifying appearance that are experienced in general by bardo beings. The first of these terrifying appearances is called 'the fear of remaining in darkness'. Driven by an intense fear of remaining in a state of perpetual darkness, the bardo being searches desperately for light. Occasionally the bardo being is able to escape the darkness and reach a place where there is light, only to see terrifying beings; this appearance is called 'the fearful appearance of demons'. The bardo being may also experience the horror of being chased and seized by these terrifying beings; this is called 'the terrifying appearance of being seized by demons'.

Since most of us have never seen anything so frightening it may be difficult for us to imagine the terror of a bardo being when confronted by such demonic beings. However, we can have similar experiences in our nightmares. Like a dreamer who totally identifies with his dream body, a bardo being totally identifies with its bardo body. Death is the cessation of the connection between the body and mind, so for as long as the body and mind of a bardo being are conjoined, it is a living being. It believes that its bardo body is its real body, that it is alive, and that its experiences are real; and it feels no connection with its previous life.

Beings in the bardo also experience a state of constant flux and uncertainty. Unable to stay in one place for very long, they have to move about from moment to moment; this is called 'the uncertainty of place'. Even if a bardo being makes contact with other bardo beings it has no choice over how long it can remain with them; this is called 'the uncertainty of friends'. The environment of a bardo being is constantly changing, such that an apparently peaceful setting can quickly turn into a dangerous and frightening one; this is called 'the uncertainty of appearance'.

In the bardo, those who previously led a non-virtuous life feel as if they are falling headlong downwards from darkness to darkness. Out of this darkness arise dreadful hallucinations that cause the bardo being great fear and misery. Bardo beings experience four terrifying sounds: (1) due to the changed appearance to the mind of the earth element they hear a sound like the thunderous collapse of a huge, rocky mountain, and they become frightened and feel as if they are being crushed beneath a falling mass; (2) due to the changed appearance to the mind of the water element they hear a sound like the huge waves of an ocean, and they become frightened and feel as if they are being carried away by the tide; (3) due to the changed appearance to the mind of the fire element they hear a sound like a fire raging in all four directions, and they become frightened and feel as if they are trapped in the midst of a fire; and (4) due to the changed appearance to the mind of the wind element they hear a sound like a violent storm, and they become frightened and feel as if they are being swept away in a whirlwind.

Bardo beings who are about to take rebirth in hell see hideous beings who appear as torturers. Just to behold them brings unbearable fear and suffering. The bardo beings are terrorized by these torturers and they hear them urging one another on, saying 'Beat him, kill him.' Hearing these words, the bardo beings panic and feel as if they are being seized and carried away by these violent executioners.

Those who have led a virtuous life experience joy in the bardo. They feel as if they are ascending from joy to joy and everything appears pervaded by moonlight. Those who are going to take human rebirth feel as if they are floating forwards, and those who are going to take rebirth as gods feel as if they are floating upwards in space.

Someone who has led a virtuous life will die peacefully and gently and will not experience disturbing hallucinations, but someone who has led a non-virtuous life will experience fearful hallucinations at the time of death and in the bardo. There was once a Tibetan aristocrat who was the manager of the prayer festival, and every year he stole tea that had been offered to the monks. Tibetan tea comes in small, hard blocks before it is broken up to make the brew. When the aristocrat was about to die, he hallucinated hundreds and hundreds of blocks of tea crushing him to death.

Those who have led a non-virtuous life experience intense fear and suffering in the bardo. We should make constant prayers to be free from the terrifying pathways of the bardo, and avoid creating the causes for such experiences.

UNDERSTANDING REBIRTH

'Rebirth' in this context means uncontrolled rebirth, the nature of which is suffering. Human beings experience human suffering because they have taken human rebirth, animals experience animal suffering because they have taken animal rebirth, and so on. Samsaric rebirth is the basis from which all the sufferings of the six realms arise.

The main causes of taking rebirth are our own actions, our accumulated throwing karma. The secondary, or co-operative, causes of rebirth – the conditions of rebirth – are of two kinds, distant and close. The distant condition is the karma of our parents to have us as their child. Examples of close conditions are our parents having sexual intercourse, and the sperm and ovum joining in our mother's womb. All these causes and conditions must come together for there to be rebirth.

If a bardo being is to take a human rebirth it circles closer and closer to the place of rebirth like a fly circling around meat. It comes closer to the home of its new parents, to the room, to the bed. When the bardo being sees its new parents copulating it develops a strong desire to join in. If it is to be female it tries to embrace the father, and if it is to be male it tries to embrace the mother; but its desire is frustrated and so it dies in anger. As it dies, the bardo being experiences all the signs of death very rapidly; and when the clear light of death ceases, its consciousness enters the union of the sperm and ovum inside the mother's womb. It enters by passing through the mouth of the father, descending to the sex organ, and then emerging through the sex organ into the mother's womb. The first moment after conception only black appears to the mind of the new human being, and then all the remaining signs of dying are experienced in reverse order as the consciousness becomes more and more gross. At first, the body in the mother's womb is liquid, like reddish-coloured yoghurt. It gradually hardens, and after a few weeks it resembles a fish. A few weeks later it resembles a turtle, and then a lion. Eventually, the body resembles a human being. After nine months and ten days the baby is born.

Some of the explanations in this book have been extracted from my other books. Even if you have read these books you should not think that it is not necessary to read these sections again. These explanations are not given for the purpose of mere intellectual understanding but to help us gain deep realizations. We need to read them again and again to become completely familiar with them. We would never think that because we ate yesterday we do not need to eat today! To maintain a healthy body we need to eat every day, and, similarly, to maintain our knowledge of Dharma and gain realizations we need to read, contemplate, and meditate on Dharma over and over again.

How to Benefit the Dying and Those Who Have Died

How to apply the practice of powa for the benefit of others has two main divisions:

1 Benefiting the deceased
2 Benefiting those who are about to die

BENEFITING THE DECEASED

This has two parts:

1 Benefiting the deceased through the practice of powa
2 Benefiting the deceased by means of prayer and dedication

BENEFITING THE DECEASED THROUGH
THE PRACTICE OF POWA

As practitioners we may be approached by the relatives or friends of someone who has recently died and requested to perform rituals on their behalf. There are extensive ritual practices (Tib. *Lhogo*) that can be performed in conjunction with the self-initiation practices of Highest Yoga Tantra, and shorter practices that can be performed by anyone. The simple practice presented here is based on the sadhana, *Path of Compassion for the Deceased*, which can be found in Appendix II. It is traditionally done within forty-nine days of a death.

To prepare for this ritual practice we begin by arranging offerings and other necessities. Whether the offerings are

Buddha Glorious Light

Buddha Glorious One
without Sorrow

Buddha Son
without Craving

small or extensive will depend upon the amount dedicated by the relatives of the deceased. Using the money of the deceased person is a powerful method for increasing his or her merit, and for enabling him or her to make a special connection with the holy beings.

On a piece of paper we draw a lotus. In the centre of this we write in red ink the initial letter of the deceased's first name, and draw a canopy above it. We attach the paper to a stick to resemble a flag, and place this name-flag in a suitable container such as a small vase. In front of this we place a photograph or drawing of the deceased to symbolize his or her presence.

On a saucer we arrange a tablespoon of black sesame seeds in the shape of a scorpion, and we prepare a fire in a small container, preferably using charcoal. The name-flag, sesame seeds, and fire should be arranged on a table in front of our seat. Finally, we stand a small candle on a saucer in front of the photograph of the deceased.

Now with a mind of strong compassion for all sentient beings in general, and for the deceased in particular, we begin the sadhana. This has two parts:

1 Self-generation
2 The actual practice

SELF-GENERATION

We engage in self-generation as Avalokiteshvara following the seven stages of the first part of the sadhana:

1 Going for refuge and generating bodhichitta
2 Generating the four immeasurables
3 Self-generation as Avalokiteshvara
4 Offerings to the self-generation
5 Praise
6 Mantra recitation
7 Dedication

THE ACTUAL PRACTICE

This has three parts:

1 Generating the deceased as a living person
2 Purifying the negative karma of the deceased
3 Transferring the consciousness of the deceased to the Pure Land

GENERATING THE DECEASED AS A LIVING PERSON

Having generated ourself as Avalokiteshvara, the Buddha of compassion, light rays radiate from the letter HRIH at our heart and reach the symbolic form of the deceased, which melts into light and becomes empty.

We imagine that from the state of emptiness the deceased appears in living aspect. Their body is in the nature of light, and their hands are folded in the gesture of prayer. Understanding that the deceased's consciousness must be in one of the three realms of existence – the desire realm, form realm, or formless realm – we again radiate light from our heart throughout all three realms. We imagine that the light hooks the deceased's consciousness and, drawing it back, dissolves it into the heart of the person generated in front. We then imagine that the living person is sitting in front of us.

PURIFYING THE NEGATIVE KARMA OF THE DECEASED

Before we can transfer the deceased's consciousness to the Pure Land we need to purify it of all the negative karma accumulated over countless previous lives. We do this in conjunction with the burning offering practice of Vajradaka, an enlightened Deity whose function is to purify the negative karma of living beings through wrathful actions.

With divine pride of ourself as Avalokiteshvara, the Buddha of compassion, we radiate light rays from the letter HRIH at our heart to the heart of the person generated in front. This causes all the negative karmic imprints that they have accumulated throughout countless lives to leave their body through the nostrils in the form of countless tiny scorpions, which dissolve into the sesame seed scorpion in front.

Then, focusing on the fire and recognizing that it is empty of existence from its own side, we imagine that from the state of emptiness there appears a wisdom fire in the aspect of the enlightened Deity Vajradaka, who has a wide-open mouth.

While reciting the mantra of Vajradaka we throw the sesame seeds – the nature of the deceased's negative karma – into the fire, and imagine that Vajradaka is consuming them. With each recitation of the mantra we throw one pinch of sesame seeds into the fire using the thumb and ring finger of our right hand. After every seventh recitation we make a heartfelt prayer for the deceased to be purified of all negativity. We continue in this way until all the sesame seeds have been burnt.

TRANSFERRING THE CONSCIOUSNESS OF THE DECEASED TO THE PURE LAND

This has seven parts:

1 Visualization
2 The three awarenesses
3 Prayer of seven limbs
4 Short mandala offering
5 Requests
6 The actual meditation
7 Dedication

VISUALIZATION

We visualize the body of the deceased in the nature of light, translucent like a rainbow. On the crown of their head is Guru Avalokiteshvara, the synthesis of all Buddhas. At Guru

Avalokiteshvara's heart the Dharmakaya of all Buddhas appears in the form of an oval-shaped jewel of white light, the size of a thumb. This is Guru Avalokiteshvara's mind. We meditate on this visualization for a while.

Then, in the centre of the deceased's body, midway between the shoulders but closer to the back than the front, we visualize their central channel. It is translucent, the nature of red light, and the width of an arrow. It begins four finger-widths below their navel and ascends through the middle of their body to their crown. It is soft and pliant, and very straight. Its lower tip is thin and solid, like the tail of a snake, but as it ascends it becomes wider and hollow. At their crown its upper tip joins the lower door of Avalokiteshvara.

Inside the central channel of the deceased, at their heart, we visualize their mind in the form of a sparkling white drop of light with a reddish tint, about the size of a pea.

We now mentally analyze all the aspects of this visualization and try to perceive them clearly. We start with their body of light, then check their central channel, their mind drop, Guru Avalokiteshvara on the crown of their head, and at his heart the Dharmakaya of all Buddhas in the form of an oval-shaped jewel of white light. We then check in reverse order, from the oval-shaped jewel of light at Guru Avalokiteshvara's heart to their body of light. We repeat this checking meditation in serial and reverse orders until we perceive a generic image of the entire visualization, and we then meditate on this without distraction.

THE THREE AWARENESSES

We then develop three awarenesses: (1) the mind of the deceased, the drop, is a traveller going to the Pure Land; (2) their central channel is the pathway to the Pure Land; and (3) the Dharmakaya of all Buddhas at Avalokiteshvara's heart is their destination.

PRAYER OF SEVEN LIMBS AND SHORT
MANDALA OFFERING

With these special awarenesses, as the representative of the deceased we offer the prayer of seven limbs and a short mandala offering to Avalokiteshvara on their crown, recognizing that he is the synthesis of all Buddhas and the same nature as our Spiritual Guide.

REQUESTS

We then make the following requests from the depths of our heart:

O Guru Avalokiteshvara, synthesis of all direct and
lineage Gurus,
I request you to dispel all . . . 's outer and inner
obstacles.
Please bless him/her to complete the profound path
of transference,
And lead him/her to the supreme Pure Land of
Buddha.

O Guru Avalokiteshvara, synthesis of all Deities,
I request you to dispel all . . . 's outer and inner
obstacles.
Please bless him/her to complete the profound path
of transference,
And lead him/her to the supreme Pure Land of
Buddha.

O Guru Avalokiteshvara, synthesis of all Buddha
Jewels,
I request you to dispel all . . . 's outer and inner
obstacles.
Please bless him/her to complete the profound path
of transference,
And lead him/her to the supreme Pure Land of
Buddha.

O Guru Avalokiteshvara, synthesis of all Dharma Jewels,
I request you to dispel all . . . 's outer and inner obstacles.
Please bless him/her to complete the profound path of transference,
And lead him/her to the supreme Pure Land of Buddha.

O Guru Avalokiteshvara, synthesis of all Sangha Jewels,
I request you to dispel all . . . 's outer and inner obstacles.
Please bless him/her to complete the profound path of transference,
And lead him/her to the supreme Pure Land of Buddha.

O Guru Avalokiteshvara, synthesis of all objects of refuge,
I request you to dispel all . . . 's outer and inner obstacles.
Please bless him/her to complete the profound path of transference,
And lead him/her to the supreme Pure Land of Buddha.

THE ACTUAL MEDITATION

We imagine that as a result of our single-pointed requests, from the oval-shaped jewel of white light – the Dharmakaya of all Buddhas at Avalokiteshvara's heart – a hook of white light descends through the deceased's central channel and reaches the mind drop at their heart. As it hooks the drop we make the sound 'HIC', and imagine with strong concentration that the mind drop ascends from the heart of the deceased to the centre of their throat chakra.

As we make the second HIC we imagine that the drop ascends to the centre of their crown chakra, and as we make the third HIC we imagine that it instantaneously enters the lower door of Avalokiteshvara and, reaching his heart, dissolves inseparably into the Dharmakaya, the inner Pure Land of Buddha. We strongly believe that the deceased has now taken rebirth in the Pure Land of Buddha, and we meditate on this conviction without distraction for as long as possible.

Having transferred the consciousness of the deceased to the Buddha Land, we imagine that their body in front of us dissolves into the name-flag. We then light the candle and think it is the nature of emptiness. From the state of emptiness appears a five-coloured wisdom fire, the nature of the five Buddha families. We hold the name-flag over the candle while chanting the mantra of Avalokiteshvara, OM MANI PÄME HUM. As the wisdom fire burns the name-flag, we imagine that the body of the deceased is purified and that they attain a Buddha's Form Body.

DEDICATION

We conclude by dedicating all our past, present, and future merit, and the merit of this practice in particular, to the deceased's attainment of full enlightenment.

There is another powa ritual practice to benefit those who have died, which is based on the sadhana *Offering to the Spiritual Guide* (Tib. *Lama Chöpa*). A detailed explanation of this can be found in *Great Treasury of Merit*.

BENEFITING THE DECEASED BY MEANS OF PRAYER AND DEDICATION

If we are requested to perform a funeral rite for someone who has recently died, we can use the sadhana *Heartfelt Prayers*, which can be found in Appendix II. This is a funeral service in which spiritual practitioners gather together to make heartfelt prayers and dedications for the deceased person to take a fortunate rebirth. The prayers set out in this ritual are only the basis for a funeral service and may be adapted as appropriate.

In general, prayers made by an assembly of many practitioners are very powerful and cannot be compared to the prayers of one or two people. The scriptures give the analogy of a broom. If we try to clean a floor with a few bristles we shall make little progress, but if we gather many bristles to make a broom we shall be successful.

This practice has two parts:

1 Accumulating a great collection of merit and wisdom
2 Dedicating this collection to the benefit of the deceased

ACCUMULATING A GREAT COLLECTION OF MERIT AND WISDOM

We can accumulate a great collection of merit and wisdom by making extensive offerings to the holy beings and contemplating the *Prayer of the Stages of the Path to Enlightenment*. The power of our prayers depends upon the strength and purity of our intention. In this service it is very important for everyone to have a mind of compassion for all living beings in general, and for the deceased in particular. If we have a genuinely compassionate motivation our prayers will definitely be effective.

Many religious people, whether Buddhist or non-Buddhist, understand the efficacy of prayer through their own experience. Prayer is by nature intention or aspiration, and so it is essentially a mental action. The words of a prayer help us to concentrate our mind and evoke faith, but they are not the actual prayer itself. Indeed, we can pray without reciting any words. The important thing is to concentrate without distraction on the meaning of the prayers as we recite them. Because we are Buddhists we make prayers in front of an image of Buddha or a visualized assembly of Buddhas, regarding them as living Buddhas. Prayers made in front of such holy beings have great power to achieve their desired effect.

DEDICATING THIS COLLECTION TO THE BENEFIT OF THE DECEASED

Dedication is defined as a prayer that observes our own or others' virtue and directs it towards a particular aim. In this context we dedicate our virtue to the benefit of the deceased. For example, if after making extensive offerings on behalf of a deceased person we pray 'Through the merit of these offerings may . . . be reborn in the Pure Land of a Buddha and attain enlightenment', this is a dedication. All virtuous actions lead to beneficial effects, and the function of dedication is to determine precisely which type of beneficial effect a particular virtuous action will produce. Virtuous actions are like a good horse, and dedication is like the reins with which to steer the horse. With a compassionate motivation our dedication will most definitely be effective.

When Buddha Shakyamuni was a Bodhisattva he accumulated a vast amount of merit by making extensive offerings and practising giving. His Spiritual Guide predicted that as a result of this vast accumulation of merit he would enjoy the wealth of a chakravatin king for many aeons. Instead, however, he dedicated all this merit so that when he became a Buddha none of his pure followers would ever die of hunger. Since then thousands of pure practitioners have benefited from Buddha's dedication.

Tibet was a very poor country, and many practitioners chose to live in the most inhospitable and inaccessible areas to engage in spiritual practice, but not one ever died of starvation. In all the countries where Buddhadharma has flourished, such as Tibet, China, India, and Mongolia, there is not a single case of a pure Dharma practitioner dying of starvation. Even in a place stricken with famine where many ordinary people die of hunger, pure practitioners miraculously find food. Just as this has happened in the past, so for as long as Buddha's doctrine remains in this world it will continue to happen in the future. This is an example of someone dedicating their virtuous actions of giving to others, and others receiving the benefits of that dedication.

The Kadampa Geshes used to say that when someone abandons attachment to wealth, wealth descends upon them like birds descending from the sky. Just as birds do not come from one particular direction but gather from all sides, so if we mentally renounce wealth it will come naturally from many different sources. This was the experience of the Kadampa Geshes.

After the Chinese invasion of Tibet, a Geshe from Sera Monastery, called Thubten Tashi, fled from Tibet to Nepal. While travelling through Tibet he was able to beg for his food, but when he came to Nepal he found himself with nothing to eat. However, instead of becoming discouraged he thought: 'Until now I have been attached to my body and cared for it unceasingly, but I have received no lasting benefit. It would be better if I completely renounced attachment to my body and enjoyments, and used the rest of my life to practise Dharma purely and prepare for my next life.' With this thought he left the town he was staying in and went up into the mountains, where he found a disused shepherd's hut. Since he had no food he did not expect to live for more than a few days, but he was not afraid and used his time to practise the yoga of Buddha Shakyamuni and the six preparatory practices of Lamrim. After a few days some shepherds appeared outside his hut and asked what he was doing there. He replied that he was there to die and would be dead within a week.

A week later the shepherds returned and found him alive and well, and not even hungry. They spread the news that an unusual man was living in the mountains. An old woman heard this and, thinking that he might be a Yogi who could give her some advice, climbed up to his hut. On seeing her the Geshe immediately asked 'Have you been having bad dreams?' He did not intend to say this, the words just came out of his mouth. She had in fact come to ask about some disturbing dreams she had recently experienced. Taken aback, she replied 'How did you know I came to see you about my dreams? You must be a Buddha.' Later she told all the villagers that a Buddha was living in the mountains, and his reputation quickly spread. Many people brought him food and asked his advice. He performed several successful divinations and became known as Dri Rinpoche. I met this Geshe personally and he told me that a pure Dharma practitioner would not be able to die of hunger even if he or she tried to do so! This story demonstrates the power of Buddha Shakyamuni's dedication.

There is no doubt that if we dedicate our virtue with the pure motivation of compassion we can definitely benefit those who have died. A dedication made by a large group of practitioners is a particularly powerful method for benefiting the deceased. Our prayers and dedications can definitely prevent the deceased from taking a lower rebirth and lead him or her to a higher rebirth, such as the Pure Land of a Buddha.

This is a general explanation that can be followed by anyone; but for a deceased person who was believed to be a highly realized being a different ritual may be more suitable. In such cases the assembly of practitioners first gathers a great collection of merit and wisdom through engaging in the ritual practice of *Offering to the Spiritual Guide*. They then dedicate this collection of virtue to the fulfilment of the deceased's wishes – for Buddhadharma to flourish throughout the world, and for living beings to find the opportunity to enter the paths of the Bodhisattva, progress through all their stages, and finally attain full enlightenment.

BENEFITING THOSE WHO ARE ABOUT TO DIE

When we know that someone is close to death we can practise powa on their behalf.

First we generate compassion by contemplating their suffering and how they have no choice over their next rebirth.
Immediately after death they will experience the fears and
suffering of the bardo. If they then take rebirth as a human
being they will have to experience all the various human
sufferings, if they are reborn as an animal they will have to
experience the sufferings of an animal, and so forth. Contemplating their suffering, from the depths of our hearts we pray:

*How wonderful it would be if this person were free from
samsaric rebirth. I myself will make this happen.*

With this mind of compassion we then engage in the powa
sadhana, *Path of Compassion for the Dying*, while deeply
contemplating its meaning. This sadhana can be found in
Appendix II.

Generally, when someone is close to death it is very
important not to touch any part of their body other than
the crown. By touching their crown we shall cause the door
of their crown chakra to open, and this will enable their
consciousness to leave the body through the crown, thereby
leading it to a higher rebirth. If the consciousness leaves
through any of the lower doors of the body it will take
rebirth in one of the lower realms. Understanding this is
very important.

Also, while the dying person is still able to hear and
understand what we are saying it is very important to keep
their mind calm and peaceful, to encourage them, and to
prevent them from becoming upset or unhappy. In this way
they will die peacefully, without any disturbance.

If the dying person is a spiritual practitioner we can
remind them of their daily practice, or at least recite or chant
their daily prayers and mantras for them. We can also remind
them of their Spiritual Guide in whom they have faith.

PART TWO

Integrating the Five Forces into the Practice of Powa

Buddha Glorious Flower

*Buddha Clearly Knowing
through Enjoying
Pure Radiance*

*Buddha Clearly Knowing
through Enjoying
Lotus Radiance*

Motivation and Familiarity

In the ritual prayer of *Offering to the Spiritual Guide* the first Panchen Lama says:

> If by the time of my death I have not completed the path,
> I seek your blessings to go to the Pure Land
> Through the instruction on correctly applying the five forces,
> The supremely powerful method of transference to Buddhahood.

For our powa practice to be most effective we need to combine it with the five forces, which are special methods that cause our practice to bear fruit. The five forces are:

1 The force of motivation
2 The force of familiarity
3 The force of white seed
4 The force of destruction
5 The force of aspirational prayer

The first force, the force of motivation, is developing and sustaining a strong wish to take rebirth in the Pure Land of a Buddha. To fulfil this wish we need to become completely familiar with the practice of powa through repeated training; this is the force of familiarity. The success of our training will depend to a large extent on our accumulating a vast collection of merit by training in virtue. This is the force of white seed, so called because we are gathering the inner conditions for seeds of virtue to ripen in our mind.

To be reborn in a Buddha's Pure Land we also need to purify all the non-virtuous actions we have accumulated over countless previous lives; this is the force of destruction. Finally, we need constantly to dedicate all our merit to the attainment of our final goal, the Pure Land of a Buddha; this is the force of aspirational prayer. Integrating the five forces into our practice of powa will enable us to complete our practice and successfully transfer our consciousness to a Buddha's Pure Land.

THE FORCE OF MOTIVATION

The first step in attaining the Pure Land is developing the wish to go there, which is the force of motivation. We need to cultivate and improve this wish until it arises spontaneously. The stronger our wish to go to the Pure Land, the more effort we shall apply, and with effort we can definitely accomplish our goal. If we are lazy we shall accomplish nothing.

From a Dharma point of view, not wanting to put effort into a virtuous task is considered to be laziness. Indeed, it is the laziness of attachment to worldly pleasure that keeps us wandering in samsara experiencing endless suffering, while the Buddhas, who applied great effort on the spiritual path, enjoy the ultimate freedom and happiness of full enlightenment.

There was once a Tibetan Yogi called Drugpa Kunleg, who went to Lhasa to pay homage to the statue of Buddha Shakyamuni at the main temple. Upon arriving in front of the statue he prostrated to it, saying:

O Buddha, to begin with you and I were exactly the
    same,
But later you attained Buddhahood through the
    force of your effort,
Whereas due to my laziness I remain in samsara;
So now I must prostrate to you.

What is a Pure Land? A Pure Land is a place in which there is a complete absence of contaminated objects, environments, and enjoyments. There is no sickness, ageing, uncontrolled death, or uncontrolled rebirth; and since there is no samsaric rebirth there are no sufferings, problems, fears, or dangers. Beings who live there have pure bodies and pure minds, and experience permanent inner peace. It is almost the same as having attained liberation, or nirvana.

Practitioners seeking permanent liberation from suffering normally need to progress through five spiritual paths – the paths of accumulation, preparation, seeing, meditation, and No More Learning – and this can take many lifetimes of sustained practice. On the other hand, powa practitioners can attain permanent freedom from suffering within a few minutes by transferring their consciousness to the Pure Land of a Buddha at the time of death. This is why it is said that powa is the method for attaining enlightenment instantaneously.

Actual liberation, or nirvana, is the ultimate nature of a mind that is completely free from delusions. There are three levels of liberation: the great liberation of a Buddha, the middling liberation of a Solitary Realizer, and the small liberation of a Hearer. Those who have attained liberation are known as 'Foe Destroyers' because they have completely destroyed the enemy of delusions. Strictly speaking, enlightenment is not necessarily a Buddha's enlightenment because it too has three levels: the great enlightenment of a Buddha, the middling enlightenment of a Solitary Realizer, and the small enlightenment of a Hearer. From this point of view, whoever has attained liberation has also attained enlightenment.

If a powa practitioner who has not entered the path to liberation applies his practice as he is dying and takes rebirth in the Pure Land of a Buddha, it is almost as if he has attained liberation. This does not mean, however, that he has completely abandoned his delusions. He still has

delusions, such as self-grasping, but their power is subdued by his pure mind. His delusions are not manifest but
their seeds still remain in his mental continuum. Once someone attains the Pure Land of a Buddha they will never again
take samsaric rebirth, but this does not necessarily mean
that they will attain actual liberation or Buddhahood quickly.

It is not difficult to see the benefits we personally shall
derive from being reborn in a Buddha's Pure Land, but how
will our taking rebirth there also help other living beings?
When we meditate on compassion we develop a heartfelt
wish to release all living beings from the relentless suffering
of samsara, but without our first attaining liberation from
samsara how can we release others? How can one drowning person save another? Thinking in this way we conclude:

*I must attain permanent liberation from samsara by taking
rebirth in the Pure Land of a Buddha, for then I shall have
the ability actually to release other living beings from samsara.*

We meditate on this determination without distraction for
as long as possible.

Realizing the immense benefits for both ourself and others
of taking rebirth in the Pure Land of a Buddha we develop
a strong wish to go there, and we then maintain this wish
day and night. Eventually this wish will become effortless
and completely natural. Every morning when we wake up
we should remember our wish to go to the Pure Land; and,
using mindfulness and alertness, we should then check our
mind throughout the day to ensure that we do not forget.
We should not allow ourself to become distracted by worldly
affairs but always keep part of our mind on this intention.

THE FORCE OF FAMILIARITY

To fulfil our wish to reach the Pure Land of a Buddha we
need to gain deep familiarity with powa practice; this is the
force of familiarity. With familiarity even the most difficult
task can become easy. For example, learning to drive or use

a computer can appear difficult to start with, but as we master the basic steps and practise on a regular basis they gradually become effortless and natural. Similarly, at the beginning we may find both the preliminaries and the actual meditations of the powa practice difficult, but as we become more and more familiar with them through daily practice they become easy and natural. We shall then be able to practise powa during our sleep; and finally, as we are dying, we shall easily transfer our consciousness to a Pure Land.

In the Lamrim teachings there is a story of an old woman whose cow died giving birth to a calf. Every morning the woman would carry the calf out into the garden for some grass and sunshine, and every evening she would carry it back indoors. She continued doing this for so long, and became so familiar with it, that even when the calf had become a fully grown cow she was still able to carry it in and out of the house. With familiarity anything is possible!

To become completely familiar with powa practice we need to exert a lot of effort, and this means practising on a regular basis. If possible we should do a session every four hours, making six sessions in a twenty-four hour period. For example, we could start the first session at 6am, the second at 10am, the third at 2pm, then at 6pm, 10pm, and 2am. We then start again at 6am, and so on.

In between sessions we should try not to forget our experience of the meditation, and we should repeatedly engage in the practices of accumulating merit and making dedications for attaining the Pure Land of a Buddha. We should also continually receive blessings from all the enlightened beings through sincere reliance upon our Spiritual Guide. In the scriptures it says that when a disciple sincerely relies upon his or her Spiritual Guide, even without invitation all the enlightened beings enter into and abide in that Spiritual Guide's body and accept the disciple's respect, devotion, and offerings. In this way the disciple receives the blessings of all the holy beings through his or her Spiritual Guide.

If we practise like this we shall gain deep experience of powa and be able to apply it without obstacles as we are dying, at which point we shall have accomplished our final goal.

As mentioned earlier, it is especially important to gain complete familiarity with the feeling that our mind is mixed with the Dharmakaya, the inner Pure Land of Buddha. In the final part of powa meditation our mind drop dissolves into Avalokiteshvara's mind. Since Avalokiteshvara's mind is the nature of great bliss, we imagine that we also are experiencing great bliss. We then stop all appearance of conventional objects so that we perceive nothing other than empty space. We regard this empty space as emptiness of inherent existence, and we feel that our mind of bliss mixes with this emptiness. Imagining that we are experiencing the union of bliss and emptiness of the Dharmakaya, we hold this feeling single-pointedly for as long as possible. To deepen our experience of this meditation we need to improve our understanding of the emptiness of all phenomena. Once we become completely familiar with this experience we shall definitely be able to transfer our consciousness to the Pure Land as we are dying.

Training in Virtue

Training in powa meditation is like sowing seeds in the field of our consciousness; but whether the crop – our attainment of the Pure Land – will ripen or not depends upon gathering the necessary conditions of merit and blessings. Just as the growth of ordinary seeds depends upon adequate nutrients and moisture in the soil, so the growth of white seeds of virtue depends upon sufficient merit and blessings in our mind. Merit and blessings give our mind the power to sustain the growth of virtue and ensure that it ripens as the desired result. A mind with little or no merit and blessings is like poor soil; even though we may be familiar with powa meditation our mind will be too weak to generate realizations, and we shall encounter many obstacles. If on the other hand we enrich our mind with merit and blessings we shall have no difficulty in fulfilling our wish to take rebirth in the Pure Land of a Buddha. Gathering the necessary conditions for the seeds of virtue to grow in our mind is the force of white seed.

To accumulate merit we need to train in virtue. What is virtue? It is a phenomenon whose main function is to produce happiness. Material objects such as gifts, money, or food may produce temporary happiness, but, depending on how we use them, may also produce suffering, and so we cannot say that their *main* function is to produce happiness. A virtuous phenomenon, however, can only cause happiness; it can never cause pain.

We need to cultivate and increase eleven types of virtuous mind. These are:

1 Faith
2 Sense of shame
3 Consideration for others
4 Non-attachment
5 Non-hatred
6 Non-ignorance
7 Effort
8 Mental suppleness
9 Conscientiousness
10 Equanimity
11 Non-harmfulness

FAITH

As Bodhisattva Shantideva says, Buddhadharma is the only medicine that can cure the diseases of the delusions and thereby free us from suffering. However, if we have no faith in Dharma we shall never develop a sincere wish to practise it; and if we do not practise Dharma there is no other method for solving our daily problems, which arise from delusions such as attachment, anger, jealousy, and ignorance. Our problems will never end by themselves, and we shall have to experience continuous suffering in life after life.

Faith is the root of spiritual realizations. Without faith our mind is like a burnt seed, for just as a burnt seed cannot germinate, so knowledge without faith can never produce Dharma realizations, and in particular Tantric realizations. Faith in Dharma induces a strong intention to practise it, and this in turn induces effort. With effort we can accomplish anything.

No matter how hard we study, if we have no faith in Dharma our intellectual knowledge will never help us to reduce our delusions, the root of all suffering. We may even become proud of our knowledge, thereby actually increasing our delusions. Dharma knowledge without faith will not help us to purify our negativity. We may even create heavy negative karma by using holy Dharma for money, reputation, power, or political authority.

If we develop faith in Dharma we shall also develop faith in Buddha – the source of Dharma, and in Sangha – the guides who assist us with our Dharma practice. If we rely sincerely upon these Three Jewels with faith and conviction we are true Buddhists.

To develop and increase our faith in Dharma we need a special way of listening and studying. For example, when we are reading a book of pure Dharma teachings we should think:

This book is like a mirror that reflects all the faults of my body, speech, and mind. By showing up all my shortcomings it provides me with a great opportunity to overcome them and thereby remove all faults from my mental continuum.

This book is supreme medicine. Through practising the instructions contained within it I can cure myself of the diseases of the delusions, which are the real source of all my problems and suffering.

This book is the light that dispels the darkness of my ignorance, the eyes with which I can see the actual path to liberation and enlightenment, and the supreme Spiritual Guide from whom I can receive the most profound and liberating advice.

It does not matter whether the author is famous or not – if a book contains pure Dharma it is like a mirror, like medicine, like light, and like eyes; and it is a supreme Spiritual Guide. If we always read Dharma books and listen to Dharma teachings with this special recognition, our faith and wisdom will definitely increase.

Buddha Glorious Wealth

*Buddha Glorious
Mindfulness*

*Buddha Glorious Name
of Great Renown*

SENSE OF SHAME AND CONSIDERATION FOR OTHERS

Sense of shame and consideration for others are the foundations of moral discipline, particularly the moral discipline of restraint. The practice of moral discipline is our principal protection against lower rebirth, and the main cause of higher rebirth.

Nagarjuna said that whereas enjoyments come from giving, the happiness of higher rebirth comes from moral discipline. The results of practising giving can be experienced in a higher realm or a lower realm, depending upon whether or not we practise it in conjunction with moral discipline. If we do not practise moral discipline our karma of giving will ripen in a lower realm. For example, as the result of actions of giving they accumulated in previous lives, some pet dogs have far better conditions than many humans – pampered by their owners, given special food and soft cushions, and treated like a favourite child. Despite these comforts these poor creatures have nevertheless taken rebirth in a lower life form with the body and mind of an animal. They have neither the bodily nor the mental basis to continue with their practice of giving, or any other virtuous action. They cannot understand the meaning of the spiritual path nor transform their minds. Once their previous karma of giving is exhausted through enjoying such good conditions, because they have had no opportunity to create more their enjoyments come to an end, and in a future life they will experience poverty and starvation. This is because they did not practise giving in conjunction with moral discipline and so did not create the cause for a higher rebirth.

Both sense of shame and consideration for others are characterized by a determination to refrain from engaging in negative and inappropriate actions, and from breaking vows and commitments. This determination is the very essence of moral discipline. We generate and sustain this determination by contemplating the benefits of practising moral discipline and the dangers of breaking it. In particular, we need always to remember that without moral discipline we have no chance of taking any higher rebirth, let alone rebirth in the Pure Land of a Buddha.

The difference between sense of shame and consideration for others is that with the former we avoid inappropriate actions for reasons that concern ourself whereas with the latter we avoid inappropriate actions for reasons that concern others. Thus, sense of shame restrains us from committing inappropriate actions by reminding us that it is not suitable to engage in such actions because, for example, we are a spiritual practitioner, an ordained person, a Teacher, an adult, and so on. If we think 'It is not right for me to kill insects because I am Buddhist', and then make a firm decision not to kill them, we are motivated by sense of shame. Our sense of shame guards us against committing negative actions by appealing to our conscience and to the standards of behaviour that we feel to be appropriate. If we are unable to generate sense of shame we shall find it extremely difficult to practise moral discipline.

Examples of consideration for others are holding back from saying something unpleasant because it will upset another person, or giving up fishing because of the suffering it causes the fish. We need to practise consideration whenever we are with other people by being mindful of how our behaviour might disturb them or harm them. Our desires are endless, and some of them would cause other people much distress if we acted them out. Therefore, before we act on a wish we should consider whether it will disturb or harm others, and if we think that it will we should not do it. If we are concerned for the welfare of others we shall naturally show them consideration.

Consideration for others is important for everyone, whether or not they are Buddhist. If we are considerate, others will like us and respect us, and our relationships with our family and friends will be harmonious and long-lasting. Without consideration, however, relationships quickly deteriorate. Consideration prevents others from losing faith in us, and is the basis for developing a mind of rejoicing.

Whether we are a good person or a bad person depends upon whether or not we have sense of shame and consideration for others. Without these two minds our daily behaviour will soon become negative and cause others to turn away from us. Sense of shame and consideration are like beautiful clothes that cause others to be attracted to us. Without them we are like a naked person whom everyone tries to avoid.

NON-ATTACHMENT

Non-attachment in this context is the mind of renunciation, which is the opponent of attachment. Renunciation is not a wish to abandon our family, friends, home, job, and so forth and become like a beggar; it is a mind that functions to stop attachment to worldly pleasures and that seeks liberation from samsaric rebirth.

We must learn to stop our attachment through the practice of renunciation, or it will be a serious obstacle to our taking rebirth in a Pure Land. If a powa practitioner develops attachment to his or her home, family, body, possessions, and so forth as he or she is dying, this will automatically close the door to the Pure Land. Just as a bird cannot fly if it has stones tied to its legs, so a mind cannot easily transfer to a Pure Land if it is attached to worldly possessions.

The time to practise renunciation is now, before our death. We need to reduce our attachment to worldly pleasures by realizing that they are deceptive and cannot give real satisfaction. In reality they cause us only suffering. Powa practitioners want to go to a Pure Land, but in a Pure Land there is very little opportunity to improve renunciation or compassion because there is no suffering – everything is pure. Therefore, this human life with all its suffering and problems is a great opportunity for us to improve both our renunciation and our compassion. We should not waste this precious opportunity. The realization of renunciation is the gateway through which we enter the spiritual path to liberation and enlightenment. Without renunciation it is impossible even to enter the path to enlightenment, let alone to progress along it.

To develop and increase our renunciation we should repeatedly contemplate our samsaric predicament:

Because my consciousness is beginningless, I have taken countless rebirths in samsara. I have already had countless bodies; if they were all gathered together they would fill the entire world, and all the blood and other bodily fluids that have flowed through them would form an ocean. So great has been my suffering in all these previous lives that I have shed enough tears of sorrow to form another ocean.

In every single life I have experienced the sufferings of sickness, ageing, death, being separated from those I love, and being unable to fulfil my wishes. If I do not attain permanent liberation from suffering now, I shall have to experience these sufferings again and again in countless future lives.

Contemplating this, from the depths of our heart we make a strong determination to abandon attachment to worldly pleasures and attain permanent liberation from samsaric rebirth, and we then meditate on this determination. We should do this contemplation and meditation every day.

There are two types of renunciation: renunciation in the mental continuum of a Hinayanist, and renunciation in the mental continuum of a Bodhisattva. A Bodhisattva's renunciation is a part of his or her bodhichitta. Bodhichitta is a primary mind motivated by great compassion that spontaneously wishes to attain the great liberation of a Buddha. This precious mind has two parts: an intention to release all living beings from samsaric rebirth – which is compassion, and a spontaneous wish to attain the great liberation of a Buddha – which is a type of renunciation. Thus a Bodhisattva's renunciation is motivated by compassion whereas a Hinayanist's is motivated by self-concern.

NON-HATRED

Non-hatred in this context is love, which is the opponent of hatred. Many people experience problems because their love is mixed with attachment; for such people the more their 'love' increases, the more their desirous attachment grows. If their desires are not fulfilled they become upset and angry. If the object of their attachment, such as their lover, even so much as talks to another person they may become jealous or aggressive. This clearly indicates that their 'love' is not real love but attachment. Real love can never be a cause of anger; it is the opposite of anger and can never cause problems. If we love everyone as a mother loves her dearest child there will be no basis for any problems to arise because our mind will always be at peace. Love is the real inner protection against suffering.

Love is a virtuous mind motivated by equanimity to which its object appears as beautiful or pleasant. Equanimity is a balanced mind that prevents us from developing anger and attachment by applying specific opponents. Recognizing anger and attachment to be harmful, like poison, equanimity prevents them from developing and keeps our mind peaceful. When the mind of equanimity is manifest we are very balanced and calm because we are free from the disturbing minds of attachment, anger, and other delusions.

Developing equanimity is like ploughing a field – clearing our mind of the rocks and weeds of anger and attachment. Practising love is like watering the soil, training in compassion is like sowing the seeds, and generating bodhichitta is like causing the seeds to sprout. The final harvest is the supreme state of Buddhahood, full enlightenment.

There are three kinds of love: affectionate love, cherishing love, and wishing love. Generally, whenever a mother sees or thinks of her dear child her mind lights up and she feels a warmth in her heart, a feeling that is especially strong if she is reunited with her child after a long absence. This feeling of delight and warmth is affectionate love. The mother's affection for her child gives rise to a feeling that the child is very precious and important, and this feeling is cherishing love. This in turn gives rise to a strong desire to give her child happiness, and this desire is wishing love.

We need to learn to love all living beings in these three ways. Whenever we meet anyone we should be happy to see them and try to generate a warm feeling towards them. On the basis of this feeling of affection we should develop cherishing love so that we genuinely come to feel that they are precious and important. If we cherish others in this way it will not be difficult to develop wishing love, wanting to give them happiness.

An important step in learning to love others is realizing that cherishing ourself, or selfishness, is the source of all our problems and suffering, whereas cherishing others is the source of all our happiness and peace. Understanding this, we make a strong resolve to cherish all living beings without exception, and then put this determination into practice. If from the depths of our heart we really want to do something we shall definitely do it, because we always follow our own wishes. If we want to steal we shall steal, if we want to kill we shall kill, and if we truly want to cherish others we shall definitely cherish them. The main point is to develop a strong wish to cherish others. If we deeply understand that cherishing others is of immense benefit to both ourself and others, and that selfish intentions and attitudes do nothing but harm, we shall naturally develop this wish. Actually it is not that difficult to cherish all living beings – we simply need to change our intention.

We can also develop and increase our love and affection for all living beings by remembering their great kindness towards us. Everything we have is due to the kindness of others. All temporary and ultimate happiness arises through the kindness of others. At the moment we possess a precious human body that enables us to enjoy all the pleasures and opportunities of a human life, including unique spiritual opportunities. Where does this body come from? Originally it came from the sperm and ovum of our parents, and then it grew and developed as a result of the food we ate and the care we received – all of which were directly or indirectly provided by others. Thus our body is a product of others' kindness.

It is impossible to find even the smallest experience of happiness that does not come about as a result of the kindness of others. We brought nothing with us from our previous life, but as soon as we were born we were given a home, clothing, food, and so forth, and later we received an education. Where did these things come from? From the kindness of others. All the facilities we take for granted such as houses, roads, shops, cars, schools, hospitals, and cinemas are produced solely through the kindness of others. When we travel by bus or car we take the roads for granted, but many people worked hard and at great expense to build them and make them safe for us to use. We may argue that the workers did not build the roads out of any altruistic motive but solely to earn money. However, even though they may not have worked with any intention to benefit us we nevertheless receive benefit from their actions, and from our point of view this is a kindness.

We might also argue that we are not given things for free but have to work for them. When we go shopping we have to pay, and when we eat in a restaurant we have to pay. We may have the use of a car, but we had to buy the car, and now we have to pay for petrol, tax, and insurance. No one gives us anything for free. But from where do we get this money? We might say that we earn it through our own hard work, but it is others who give us jobs, and so indirectly it is they who provide the money with which we buy our enjoyments. If we think like this we shall see that all our happiness, and indeed all happiness in the world, is the result of others' kindness.

Contemplating the innumerable ways in which others are kind to us we make a firm decision: 'I must cherish others because they are so kind to me.' Based on this determination we develop a feeling of cherishing others – a sense that others are important and that their happiness matters. We try to mix our mind single-pointedly with this feeling and maintain it for as long as we can without forgetting it. Then when we rise from meditation we carry this feeling into our everyday life, so that whenever we meet anyone we think: 'This person is important. Their happiness is important.' In this way we can make cherishing others our main practice.

Our ability to enter and make progress on the spiritual path and to attain full enlightenment also depends entirely on the kindness of other living beings; and we need to attain enlightenment because in this impure world there is no true happiness. Without living beings acting as the objects of our love and compassion it would be impossible for us to develop these minds, and without love and compassion for all living beings we shall never attain full enlightenment. Therefore all living beings are precious and important for us because they all act as the objects of our love and compassion.

It is due to the kindness of others that we have the opportunity to listen to, contemplate, and meditate on Buddha's holy teachings. Other people have provided us with all the necessary conditions for our spiritual practice. Without sentient beings to give to, to test our patience, to help, or to develop love and compassion for, we could never develop the qualities needed to become enlightened. This is why Bodhisattva Shantideva said that sentient beings are as important and precious for us as Buddhas.

Keeping this in mind we should always feel warmth and affection towards everyone we meet. Having developed affectionate love and cherishing love for all sentient beings through practising the methods explained above, we then need to engage in extensive contemplation on how sentient beings lack true happiness. In this way we shall develop wishing love, wanting all sentient beings to be happy. By contemplating the many different types of suffering that each and every sentient being has to endure we shall develop compassion – wanting to release them all from samsaric rebirth, the basis of all their suffering.

Although we see many unhappy and suffering beings we do not normally feel compassion for them because we lack affectionate love and cherishing love. The development of compassion depends totally on first developing affectionate love and cherishing love. If we truly cherish others, whenever we see or hear of their suffering, compassion arises naturally; and whenever we see or hear that they lack true happiness, we develop wishing love. Wishing love and compassion are like two sides of a coin – with wishing love we want to make others happy, and with compassion we want to release them from suffering.

NON-IGNORANCE

Non-ignorance is wisdom realizing selflessness, which is the opponent to the ignorance of self-grasping. Our self-grasping causes us to wander endlessly in samsara, the cycle of uncontrolled death, rebirth, and suffering. First we develop a conceptual mind thinking 'I' that grasps at our I as being truly existent; and then we develop a mind thinking 'mine' that grasps at other phenomena as truly existent. As a result we develop attachment for attractive objects, anger at unattractive objects, and ignorance towards neutral objects. Through the force of these delusions we create contaminated actions, or karma, which throw us into repeated samsaric rebirths. If we take a human rebirth we have to experience human problems and suffering, if we are reborn as an animal we have to experience animal suffering, and so on. If we contemplate this process of samsara sincerely and try to understand how it works we shall clearly realize that self-grasping ignorance is the root of all suffering.

If we do not want to experience problems and suffering we have to cut the continuum of our self-grasping. As the method to do this, Buddha taught how to realize selflessness, or emptiness – the lack of true existence of persons and phenomena. Persons and other phenomena have no existence from their own side but exist as mere imputation by conceptual thought. If we realize this deeply, and completely familiarize our mind with the truth of this selflessness, we can cut the continuum of our self-grasping.

The Buddhist Master Chandrakirti uses the analogy of an imagined snake to show how all phenomena are merely imputed by thought. A man walking through a field at dusk comes across a coil of speckled rope in the grass and, mistaking it for a snake, develops fear. Even though a snake appears vividly to his mind, that snake does not exist from its own side. It is merely a projection of his mind, imputed by conceptual thought in dependence upon the rope. Other than this, no snake can be found because neither the coil of rope as a whole nor any part of it is a snake.

In just the same way, all phenomena are merely imputed by conceptual thought. For example, our I does not exist from its own side. It is merely a projection of the mind imputed by conceptual thought in dependence upon our body and mind. If we try to find an I other than the mere conceptual imputation 'I' we shall not succeed, because neither the collection of our body and mind nor any individual part of our body and mind is our I. Existing phenomena such as the I differ from the imagined snake in that they are valid imputations; but there is no difference from the point of view of their being merely imputed by conceptual thought.

In the analogy, because the man sees the rope in the twilight he mistakenly apprehends a snake and develops fear. To remove this fear he must remove the mind apprehending a snake by realizing that there is no snake. Even then, if the rope is left in the same place there is a danger that the same mistake will be made in the future. The only way to remove this danger is to remove the rope. Similarly, sentient beings observing their body and mind in the darkness of their ignorance mistakenly apprehend an inherently existent I. This mind grasping at an inherently existent I is the root of samsara and the source of all fear. To remove the fears of samsara we must remove this mind by realizing that there is no inherently existent I. Even then, there will be a danger of the mind grasping at an inherently existent I recurring if we continue to grasp at our body and mind as inherently existent. Therefore, the only way to remove the fears of samsara entirely is first to realize the lack of inherent existence of the I, which is selflessness of persons, and then to realize the lack of inherent existence of other phenomena such as the body and mind, which is selflessness of phenomena.

We can use other analogies such as seeing a spider on a wall where there is only a mark, seeing a person in the distance where there is only a pile of stones, or generating fear during a film. By contemplating these analogies we can understand how all phenomena are merely imputed by thought and do not exist from the side of the object. A phenomenon's lack of existence from its own side is its emptiness and its true, or ultimate, nature. We should meditate on this emptiness.

It is helpful to consider what an inherently existent object would look like if one did indeed exist. 'Inherent existence', 'true existence', and 'existence from its own side' are synonymous. If something were inherently existent it would have an existence within itself, independent of other phenomena; if something were truly existent it would exist truly as it appears and could be found upon investigation; and if something existed from its own side its existence would be established from the side of the object itself without depending upon an apprehending consciousness. Nothing exists in any of these ways. Nothing is inherently existent, nothing is truly existent, and nothing exists from its own side.

If we are ordinary beings, all objects appear to us to exist inherently. Objects seem to be independent of our mind and independent of other phenomena. The universe appears to consist of discrete objects that have an existence from their own side. These objects appear to exist in themselves as stars, planets, mountains, people, cars, and so forth, all 'waiting' to be experienced by conscious beings. Normally it does not occur to us that we are involved in any way in the existence of these phenomena. Instead, each object appears to have an existence completely independent of us and all other objects. As we shall see, the truth is very different. The way in which objects appear is quite different from the way in which they actually exist.

We can examine the question of inherent existence in terms of our sense of self, or I. We all grasp at a self in dependence upon the collection of our body and mind, but not every apprehension we have of I is self-grasping. In apprehending I, or self, two distinct aspects of the mind are functioning. One, which is valid, apprehends the conventionally existent mere I; and the other, which is non-valid, apprehends an inherently existent I, which does not exist. The latter is the mind of self-grasping.

For ordinary beings these two modes of existence of the self, one that actually exists and the other that is completely non-existent, appear mixed together, and it is extremely difficult to tell them apart. There are times, however, when the falsely conceived I appears more vividly, such as when we are in danger, embarrassed, ashamed, or indignant. If we recall or imagine such a situation we can see that at such times we have an exaggerated sense of self. Our I appears to exist in and of itself without in any way depending upon our body or mind. For example, if we are wrongly accused of something we do not think 'They are accusing my body and mind', rather we think 'They are accusing *me*!'; and an I appears vividly to our mind, wounded and indignant.

The same is true if we are in danger. Suppose while walking in the mountains we come to a rickety bridge spanning a ravine and are afraid to cross. Our self-grasping intensifies and we have a strongly exaggerated sense of self. We are not apprehending a self that is merely imputed in dependence upon the collection of our body and mind, rather we are grasping frantically at a self that appears independent of our body and mind. We do not fear 'My body and mind might fall', but rather '*I* might fall!'

This I, or self, existing independently of body and mind is an inherently existent I. It does not exist, and the mind that conceives it is a wrong awareness. This mind is an example of self-grasping, and the I that it holds onto so strongly is the negated object of emptiness. This is not to say that there is no I at all. There is a conventionally existent I that is merely imputed by thought in dependence upon the body and mind, but it can be distinguished from the non-existent, inherently existent I only by a sharp and penetrating mind.

It is important to realize that we do not grasp at this false sense of self only in times of danger and so on. For ordinary beings there is not a single moment in which grasping at an inherently existent self is not functioning, though it is not always so intense. Even insects have this self-grasping. For example, if we put a finger in front of an ant it stops and turns away. What is going on in its mind? It fears 'Someone is harming me.' It is not clinging to either its body or its mind but to a vividly appearing self independent of body and mind. This clinging mind is the ant's self-grasping.

Although the I is dependent upon the collection of our body and mind, through the force of habitual self-grasping we hold the opposite view – it seems to us that the body and mind depend upon the I. We habitually regard our body and mind as our possessions and conceive an I that owns and controls them; thus we talk of *my* body and *my* mind. In this way we grasp at an I that is independent of body and mind, and that can appear to the mind without depending upon the appearance of the body, the mind, or any of their parts. In reality this is impossible.

What is true of the self is also true of all other phenomena – they appear to our mind to exist independently of their parts, and we habitually grasp at them as existing in this way. This grasping at phenomena other than the self as inherently existent is self-grasping of phenomena. It too is a wrong awareness, and the object it conceives, an inherently existent object, is non-existent and an object to be negated in our understanding of emptiness.

It is very important to contemplate and understand deeply the emptiness, or lack of inherent existence, of persons and phenomena. All our suffering and dissatisfaction can be traced to our clinging to the inherent existence of our self and other phenomena. To gain liberation from samsara's sufferings and attain full enlightenment we must realize that all phenomena lack inherent existence. As mentioned before, it is especially important for powa practitioners to become deeply familiar with the meditation on the feeling that our mind is mixed with the union of bliss and emptiness of the Dharmakaya, the inner Buddha Land. If we have a correct understanding of emptiness, this meditation will be more profound and qualified.

EFFORT

Effort is defined as a mind that delights in virtue. Its function is to make our mind happy to engage in virtuous actions. With effort we delight in actions such as giving, helping others, and engaging in the practices of the stages of the path to enlightenment, and here, in particular, the practice of powa. Effort is necessarily virtuous. Those who strive for ordinary goals such as business achievements, and those who delight in non-virtue, are not practising effort.

Effort is the chief opponent to laziness. There are three types of laziness: laziness arising from attachment to worldly pleasures, laziness arising from attachment to distracting activities, and laziness arising from discouragement. In general, fondness for sleep is a type of laziness, but if we are able to practise the yoga of sleeping and transform sleep into a virtuous action then the mind that enjoys sleep is effort. Similarly, if we transform other neutral actions such as working, eating, cooking, or playing into virtuous actions by performing them with a good motivation, our enjoyment of them is also effort.

Laziness deceives us and causes us to wander aimlessly in samsara. If we can break free from the influence of laziness and immerse ourself deeply in our powa training we shall quickly attain our spiritual goal. Training in powa is like constructing a large building – it demands continuous effort. If we allow our effort to be interrupted by laziness we shall never see the completion of our work.

In *Ornament for Mahayana Sutras* Maitreya lists many benefits of effort:

Among virtuous collections, effort is supreme.
With effort we can accomplish all virtuous qualities,
With effort we can accomplish a peaceful body and
    mind,
With effort we can accomplish mundane and
    supramundane attainments,
With effort we can obtain the pleasures of samsara,
With effort we can take rebirth in a Pure Land,
With effort we can be freed from delusions such as the
    view of the transitory collection, and attain liberation,
With effort we can attain great enlightenment.

Buddha King of the Victory Banner

*Buddha Glorious One
Complete Subduer*

*Buddha Great
Victor in Battle*

Effort is the supreme virtue because all virtuous qualities are attained through the power of effort. Effort makes both body and mind peaceful, comfortable, and healthy by inducing physical and mental suppleness. When we have attained physical suppleness we do not need physical exercise to keep our body flexible and healthy. By relying upon effort we can attain both mundane and supramundane attainments, such as the Highest Yoga Tantra realizations of Deities like Heruka and Vajrayogini. Even the happiness of humans or gods depends solely upon our own effort because if we do not make an effort to practise virtue we shall not be able to take such rebirths in the future. Similarly, as powa practitioners we have the opportunity to attain rebirth in a Pure Land, but whether we succeed in doing so depends upon our own effort. If we joyfully and continually engage in the methods for attaining rebirth in a Pure Land our wishes will definitely be fulfilled.

If we do not apply ourself to our spiritual practice no one can grant us liberation from suffering – not our spiritual friends, nor our Spiritual Guide, nor even all the Buddhas. We are often unrealistic in our expectations. We wish we could attain enlightenment swiftly without having to apply any effort, and we want to be happy without having to create virtuous causes. Unwilling to endure even the slightest discomfort we want all our suffering to cease, and while living in the jaws of the Lord of Death we wish to remain like a long-life god. No matter how much we long for these wishes to be fulfilled, they never will be. If we do not apply energy and effort to our spiritual practices all the hopes we have for happiness will be in vain.

We all have the seed of Buddhahood within our mental continuum, and we have the opportunity to practise the methods for ripening this seed, but our attainment of Buddhahood depends upon our own efforts. An intellectual understanding of Dharma is not sufficient to carry us to Buddhahood – we must also overcome our laziness and put our knowledge into practice. All those who have already become Buddhas have attained enlightenment through their own effort, and all those who will become Buddhas in the future will do so through their own effort. In the Sutras, Buddha says:

If you have only effort you have all Dharmas,
But if you have only laziness you have nothing.

A person who has no great knowledge of Dharma but who nevertheless applies effort consistently will gradually attain all virtuous qualities; but a person who knows a great deal and has only one fault, laziness, will not be able to increase his or her good qualities and gain experience of Dharma.

In *Guide to the Bodhisattva's Way of Life* Bodhisattva Shantideva presents four types of effort:

(1) Armour-like effort
(2) Effort of non-discouragement
(3) Effort of application
(4) Effort of non-satisfaction

All four types of effort are very important for Dharma practitioners in general, and for those who wish to train in powa in particular. The first two overcome conditions unfavourable to the practice of Dharma, the third actually engages in Dharma practice, and the fourth enables us to complete our practice.

Armour-like effort is a courageous mind that helps us to persevere in our spiritual practice no matter what hardships are involved. We can generate this effort by thinking:

I will continue to practise Dharma even if it takes me many aeons to attain great enlightenment. I will never give up my Dharma practice, no matter what difficulties I might encounter.

With armour-like effort we have a long-term perspective that prevents us from being discouraged by unfavourable external conditions, and we joyfully persevere with our practice even if it takes a long time to attain Dharma realizations. In the past when soldiers went to war they wore armour to protect their bodies; similarly when Dharma practitioners wage war against their delusions they need to wear armour-like effort to protect their minds against difficult external conditions.

We need armour-like effort at the beginning of our practice because without it we may soon become discouraged by the length of time it takes to attain realizations, and as a result we may abandon our Dharma practice. Sometimes, when we find it difficult to fulfil our spiritual expectations, or if we have friends who try to dissuade us from practising, or if we have difficulty in finding the resources to support our practice, we may consider giving up Dharma. If this happens it indicates that we lack armour-like effort. At such times we need to recall our initial enthusiasm, and strengthen our resolve by reminding ourself of the benefits of our practice.

Whereas armour-like effort protects our practice against external obstacles, the effort of non-discouragement protects us against the internal obstacle of discouragement. Sometimes we may become disheartened and think 'I can't practise Dharma. I am hopeless and always fail in whatever I do.' If we indulge in such thoughts, how can we delight in our virtuous actions? To abandon this laziness of discouragement we first reinforce our armour-like effort and then contemplate:

Sometimes my delusions are strong and sometimes they are weak. This indicates that they are impermanent. If they can be reduced temporarily, they can be eradicated altogether; so why can I not attain liberation? Buddha said that everyone has Buddha nature. If I rely sincerely upon my Spiritual Guide and practise what he or she teaches me there is no reason why I cannot attain enlightenment. With my mind empowered by my Guru's blessings I can accomplish anything.

The effort of application functions to enable us actually to engage in the practice of virtue. This effort inspires us to listen to, contemplate, and meditate on Dharma teachings. It is the source of all our understanding and experience of Dharma. This effort can be either forceful or steady. Sometimes it is appropriate to use forceful effort to reach a specific goal or to overcome a particular obstacle, but it is difficult to sustain this kind of effort and it may soon lead to tiredness or discouragement. For the most part we should practise with steady effort, like a broad river flowing constantly. We should adjust our expectations and not hope for quick results, but practise steadily and constantly over a long period.

The effort of non-satisfaction encourages us continually to deepen our understanding and experience of Dharma by not being satisfied with a merely superficial experience or understanding. After having studied Dharma for two or three years we may feel contented with our understanding and feel that we have no need to listen to more teachings or to continue to meditate. Such a complacent attitude prevents us from developing deep experience and understanding. We cannot expect great results after only a few years' practice. Until we have reached the final realizations of great enlightenment we need continuously to listen to teachings and meditate on their meaning.

This precious human body that we now possess is like a boat that can carry us across the ocean of samsaric suffering and take us to the island of enlightenment. If we extract the real meaning and value of this precious human life we can reap great benefits, but if we waste this rare opportunity how shall we ever be able to find such a precious form again? Just as a boat without a conscientious helmsman will never reach its destination, so the boat of our precious human rebirth will never cross the ocean of suffering if it is not guided by the power of Dharma. As Bodhisattva Shantideva says:

By depending upon this boat-like human form
We can cross the great ocean of suffering.
Since such a vessel will be hard to find again,
This is no time to sleep, you fool!

No matter how much effort we put into following samsaric paths we shall never experience true happiness. In our previous lives we put great effort into accumulating material wealth, but now everything we owned has vanished. Our effort was in vain. In the past we have enjoyed every conceivable samsaric pleasure, but now we have nothing to show for it. All that remain are the imprints of the negative actions we committed in fulfilling our desires. Now that we have the opportunity to follow a perfect path that leads to ultimate happiness it would be a great shame if we were to abandon it for a worldly path.

The effort we apply in our powa training will be greatly increased if we employ the four powers: the power of aspiration, the power of steadfastness, the power of joy, and the power of rejection. Our ability to practise powa depends upon our motivation; if we have a strong motivation to engage in the practice we shall do so. This is the power of aspiration. Once we begin our training we should not waver in our practice or turn away from it but complete it through the power of steadfastness. If we take delight in our training and enjoy our powa practice we have generated the power of joy, which gives our practice tremendous impetus. Finally, if we become tired we should relax our efforts by employing the power of rejection, sometimes called the 'power of rest', and then resume once our strength has returned. The term 'rejection' here refers to the elimination of our tiredness through rest, not to a rejection of our effort!

These four powers increase and complete the practice of effort. They are like a vast army of soldiers who conquer the opposing forces of laziness, one of the greatest obstacles to success in any spiritual practice. Just as a country uses its army to defeat its enemies, so our effort will defeat our enemy of laziness by employing the four powers.

MENTAL SUPPLENESS

Mental suppleness is defined as a flexibility of mind induced by virtuous concentration. Many practitioners experience problems in their meditations due to mental and physical inflexibility. They may feel mentally or physically heavy, tired, or uncomfortable. The opponent to these obstacles is mental suppleness.

We develop mental suppleness by applying effort in our meditation. Even though we may experience problems such as heaviness, tiredness, or other forms of mental or physical discomfort at the beginning of our meditation, we should nevertheless patiently persevere and try to become familiar with our practice. Gradually as our concentration improves it will induce mental suppleness; and our mind and body will feel light, healthy, and tireless, and be free from obstacles to concentration. All our meditations, including powa meditation, will become easy and effective, and we shall have no difficulty in making progress.

However difficult meditation may be at the beginning, we should never give up hope. Instead we should engage in the practice of moral discipline, which protects us from gross distractions and acts as the basis for developing pure concentration. Moral discipline also strengthens mindfulness, which is the life of concentration. In addition we should accumulate merit, purify our negative karma, and receive the blessings of the holy beings. Through gathering these necessary conditions we shall find it easy to make progress in our meditations, and in particular in our powa practice. There are many levels of mental suppleness induced by different levels of concentration, full details of which can be found in *Understanding the Mind* and *Ocean of Nectar*.

CONSCIENTIOUSNESS

This section has two parts:

1 An explanation of conscientiousness
2 An explanation of the six root delusions

AN EXPLANATION OF CONSCIENTIOUSNESS

Conscientiousness is defined as a mental factor that, in dependence upon effort, cherishes what is virtuous and guards the mind from delusion and non-virtue. There are two ways to practise conscientiousness. The first is to keep our mind free from a delusion by preventing our mind from meeting the objects of that delusion. We can, for example, prevent ourself from getting angry with someone with whom we have had a disagreement by avoiding them and not thinking about them. The second way is to prevent our mind from developing inappropriate attention when it meets with objects of delusion. Inappropriate attention causes delusions to arise by exaggerating the good or bad characteristics of an object. If we prevent inappropriate attention it is impossible for delusions to arise, even if we are directly confronted with an object of delusion. For example, if we unexpectedly meet someone with whom we normally get angry we can prevent inappropriate attention by focusing on their good qualities or by remembering the faults of anger, and in this way stop ourself from getting angry.

Conscientiousness is essential for our practice of pure moral discipline. If we are conscientious about our behaviour, our understanding and realizations will automatically increase, while the defilements of our body, speech, and mind will naturally decrease. Generally, when a conscientious person speaks he or she is polite, saying things that will benefit others as well as himself. A thoughtless person, on the other hand, speaks under the influence of delusion. His behaviour is inconsiderate, and what he says invariably upsets others and brings problems upon himself.

Being conscientious about our three doors of body, speech, and mind is the best way to ensure that our positive, virtuous qualities are stabilized and abundantly increase. If we wish to be successful in our meditation practices we must practise conscientiousness. In the *Vinaya Sutras* Buddha says that through moral discipline we shall attain concentration, and through concentration we shall attain wisdom. Since conscientiousness is the root of moral discipline, it follows that concentration and wisdom also depend upon conscientiousness. By practising conscientiousness we keep our mind pure and harnessed to virtuous objects, and so our energy is not dissipated by external or internal distractions. As a result our mind becomes settled and gathered within, making it easy for us to develop virtuous concentration. Virtuous concentration makes our mind lucid and powerful, which in turn enables us to improve our wisdom.

In *Guide to the Bodhisattva's Way of Life* Bodhisattva Shantideva says that there is no practice more important than keeping our mind free from negativity. Normally we take great care to protect our body from injury, but it is much more important to protect our mind. For example, if we are crossing a busy street we take great care to avoid being run over, but if we were to be run over the worst that could happen would be that we would lose this one life. By contrast, if we do not take care to protect our mind from negativity when we are surrounded by so many objects of delusion there is great danger of our mind being overrun by delusions, which will inflict harm on us for many future lives. Therefore, the practice of conscientiousness is of paramount importance.

Conscientiousness should be practised in conjunction with mindfulness and alertness. Mindfulness is a mental factor that focuses on an object with which the mind is already acquainted. Its nature is to hold onto its object without forgetting it, and its function is not to wander from the object it is holding. With mindfulness we tie our mind to a virtuous object. A virtuous object is any object that has a positive effect on our mind, such as the twenty-one objects of meditation presented in *The Meditation Handbook*. Without mindfulness we cannot make progress in our studies or in our practice.

The mental factor alertness is a type of wisdom that examines our mind and understands how it is functioning. For example, once we have placed our mind on an object with mindfulness, alertness checks to see if our meditation is proceeding well or badly, and whether our mind has fallen under the control of a delusion. Alertness is the fruit of mindfulness and has a very close connection with it. While mindfulness holds onto its object, alertness checks to see if there is any wandering from that object. At the beginning, middle, and end of our practice, mindfulness and alertness are of the utmost importance for attaining virtuous qualities.

We can understand how these two mental factors operate together by considering how we visualize the form of Buddha Shakyamuni. First we look at a painting or statue and try to generate a mental image of what we have seen. This mental image is the object of our visualization. Once we have found the object, our mindfulness holds onto it without wandering. When the mind remains on the object single-pointedly, this is concentration. As we maintain our concentration we occasionally check carefully to see if our meditation is progressing well, or whether interruptions and obstacles have arisen. This spy-like function of the mind is alertness. If it discovers that the mind has fallen under the influence of dullness or distraction we should once again grasp the object with mindfulness and continue our meditation.

The main function of conscientiousness is to enable us to keep pure moral discipline and improve our concentration. Through practising conscientiousness we can reduce our delusions and thereby stop committing negative actions of body, speech, and mind; and as a result we shall naturally possess pure moral discipline. If our delusions are weakened and our life becomes more disciplined we shall develop far fewer distractions, and as a result we shall find it easy to make progress in our meditations.

AN EXPLANATION OF THE SIX ROOT DELUSIONS

As mentioned above, conscientiousness is an essential practice in guarding our mind from delusions. If we cannot recognize delusions as they arise in our mind it will be impossible to apply conscientiousness. According to Dharma, our worst enemy is delusion. What exactly is a delusion? A delusion is a mental factor that arises from inappropriate attention and functions to make the mind unpeaceful and uncontrolled.

If we wish to be free from all suffering we must be able to identify the various delusions within our mind and understand how they harm us. We know who our external enemies are and what dangers they pose, but we pay little attention to the inner enemies inflicting terrible damage on our mind. If we cannot recognize our delusions, how can we ever be free from suffering?

In general there are countless delusions, but they can all be included within the six root delusions:

1 Attachment
2 Anger
3 Deluded pride
4 Ignorance
5 Deluded doubt
6 Deluded view

ATTACHMENT

Attachment is a mental factor that observes a contaminated object, feels it to be attractive, exaggerates its attractions, considers it desirable, develops a desire to possess it, and feels as if it has become absorbed into the object. It works in two ways: wishing to obtain an object, and wishing never to be separated from an object. Suppose two people have a strong wish to be together as a couple – this is an example of the first type of attachment. If they subsequently become a couple and then develop a desire never to be apart from one another, this is an example of the second type. We can also develop attachment for inanimate objects.

Under the influence of attachment our mind is absorbed into the desired object in the same way that oil is absorbed into cloth. Just as it is very difficult to separate oil from the cloth it has stained, so is it difficult to separate the mind from the object to which it is attached.

It is because of our attachment that we continue to wander in samsara experiencing endless suffering. The prerequisite for attaining liberation or full enlightenment, or even to be ordained as a monk or a nun, is the mind of renunciation; but attachment to the transitory pleasures of this world prevents us from developing renunciation. Since beginningless time we have been unable to free ourself from the prison of samsara because we have been bound by the chains of attachment. If we have a sincere wish to attain spiritual realizations we must renounce samsara, and we can do this only by reducing our attachment.

Once we have recognized our attachment we can reduce its hold on our mind by repeatedly contemplating its many faults and meditating on the unattractiveness and impurity of the desired object. However, this method is only a temporary opponent and does not permanently remove attachment from our mind. To do this we need to eradicate our self-grasping, which is the root cause not only of attachment but of all the delusions; and to eradicate self-grasping we need to meditate on the wisdom realizing emptiness. For a realization of emptiness to lead to complete liberation from suffering it must be combined with renunciation, tranquil abiding, and superior seeing. A full explanation of these subjects can be found in *Joyful Path of Good Fortune* and *Meaningful to Behold*.

ANGER

Anger is a mental factor that exaggerates the unpleasant characteristics of an object and wishes to harm it. As with attachment, anger can be directed at both animate and inanimate objects.

How does anger harm us? Buddha said that anger decreases or destroys all our accumulations of virtue and can lead us to the hell realms. A moment's anger directed at a Bodhisattva, for example, can destroy all the merit we may have accumulated to take rebirth in a higher realm.

Anger is the fire that burns the wood of our virtue. It lurks behind all disputes, whether they be domestic quarrels between husband and wife or wars between nations. Anger destroys good relationships and ruins the happiness within families, between friends, and among colleagues at work. It quickly causes us to be separated from those whom we like.

There is no evil greater than anger. It is a force capable not only of negating the effects of whatever positive actions we may have done in the past but also of preventing us from attaining goals we have set for the future, whether they be attaining enlightenment or simply improving our mind. The opponent to anger is patience, and if we really want to make genuine spiritual progress we must realize that there is no greater practice than patience.

The destruction of virtue is one of the invisible faults of anger and therefore something we must accept on faith, but there are many visible faults of this delusion. Whenever we are overcome by anger we immediately lose all peace of mind and even our body becomes uncomfortable. We are plagued by restlessness and the food we eat seems unpalatable. We find it nearly impossible to fall asleep, and, when we do, our sleep is fitful. Anger transforms a normally attractive person into an ugly red-faced demon. We grow more and more miserable, and no matter how hard we try we cannot control our feelings.

One of the most harmful effects of anger is that it robs us of our reason and good sense. We lose all freedom of choice, and driven here and there by revenge or rage we often expose ourself to great personal danger. Sometimes our anger is even directed at our loved ones and benefactors. In a fit of anger, forgetting the immeasurable kindness we have received from our friends, family, or teachers, we may shout at or even strike those we hold most dear. It is no wonder that an angry person is soon avoided by everyone who knows him or her.

We generally assume that we get angry in response to meeting someone we do not like, but in truth the situation is often the exact reverse; it is the anger already within us that transforms the person we meet into an imagined enemy. Someone who is prone to anger lives within a web of suspicion and paranoia, surrounded by enemies of his or her own creation. The false belief that others hate him can become so overwhelming that he might even go insane, the victim of his own delusion.

It often happens that in a group one person always blames the others for what goes wrong, but in fact it is generally that person who is responsible for the disharmony. There was once an old woman who used to argue and fight with everyone. She was so disagreeable that eventually she was expelled from her village. When she arrived at another village the people there asked her 'Why did you leave your previous home?' She replied 'All the people in that village were malicious and vindictive – I left there to escape from them.' The villagers thought this very strange and concluded that it must have been the woman herself who was at fault. Fearing that she would cause trouble and disharmony in their village as well, they told her to leave. The angry old woman wandered from village to village looking for somewhere to live, but no one would have her as their neighbour.

It is very important to recognize the true cause of whatever unhappiness we feel. If we are forever blaming our difficulties on others, this is a sign that there are still many problems and faults within our own mind. Why is this? If we were truly peaceful inside and had our mind under control, nothing would be able to disturb that peace and no one we met would appear to be our enemy. To someone who has subdued his or her mind and eradicated anger, everyone is a friend. A Bodhisattva, for example, whose sole concern is for the welfare of others, has no enemies. Very few people wish to harm someone who is a friend of the entire world; and even if someone did harm or abuse such a high-minded being, the Bodhisattva would remain at peace. With his or her mind dwelling in patience he would remain calm and untroubled, able to smile at his assailant and even treat him with respect. Such is the power of a well-controlled mind. Therefore, if we sincerely wish to be rid of all our enemies the wisest course of action is to uproot and destroy our own anger.

We should not think that this is an impossible task or an unreasonable goal. Skilled doctors are now able to cure illnesses that were fatal only a short time ago, and they have eradicated some diseases completely. Just as scientists and physicians fought and finally overcame these diseases, so can we eradicate the disease of anger infecting our mind. Methods to gain release from this crippling delusion are available to us all. They have proved their effectiveness whenever people have sincerely put them into practice, and there is no reason why they cannot work for us as well.

Imagine what the world would be like if we all conquered our anger! The danger of war would evaporate, armies would become unnecessary, and soldiers would have to look elsewhere for work. Guns, tanks, and bombs – instruments useful only to the angry mind – would be destroyed, as all conflicts, from wars between nations to quarrels between individuals, came to an end. Even if such universal harmony is too much to hope for, imagine the freedom and peace of mind each of us individually would enjoy if we exorcized this hateful demon within us.

Someone who always gets angry will never find happiness, either in this or future lives. Therefore, we should always remember that anger is our main enemy, the creator of so much of our suffering, and continuously strive to defeat it.

DELUDED PRIDE

Deluded pride is a mental factor that feels arrogant for slight reasons. We can use anything – our looks, our knowledge, our skills, our wealth – as a pretext for thinking that we are someone special and developing pride. We can even be proud of our Dharma understanding and feel superior to others.

Pride is harmful because it prevents us from improving ourself. A proud mind does not want to acknowledge faults, nor admit that there is room for improvement. A mind inflated with pride cannot accept fresh knowledge from a qualified Teacher. Just as water cannot collect on the top of a mountain, so knowledge cannot accumulate in a mind falsely elevated by pride.

To reduce our pride we need to contemplate how vulnerable and unfree we are. We can meditate on all the unpleasant experiences we must suffer without choice, such as birth, sickness, ageing, and death. At present we may be good-looking, fit, intelligent, and successful, but we have no power to remain like this. Eventually, without choice, we shall have to become old, sick, forgetful, or senile. If we compare ourself to realized beings who have perfect freedom and whose happiness cannot be destroyed by external conditions we shall soon lose our pride.

Not all pride is deluded pride – there are some forms of pride that we should cultivate. Non-deluded pride, or self-confidence, is essential for our spiritual progress. Thus we need to take pride in our spiritual potential and in our virtuous actions, and we need to have confidence in our

Buddha Glorious One Complete
Subduer Passed Beyond

Buddha Glorious Array   *Buddha Jewel Lotus*
Illuminating All   *Great Subduer*

ability to overcome our delusions and benefit others. Understanding the difference between these two types of pride, we should abandon deluded pride while cultivating non-deluded pride.

IGNORANCE

Ignorance is a mental factor that functions to make its primary mind confused about its object. It induces wrong awareness, doubt, and other delusions. It is like a darkness in our mind that prevents us from clearly understanding our object. An example is the confusion we experience when we are reading a book and cannot understand its meaning. The ignorance of not understanding selflessness – the ultimate nature of persons and other phenomena – induces self-grasping, or true-grasping, which is the root of all other delusions and all cyclic rebirths.

In general, there are two main types of ignorance: ignorance of karma and ignorance of emptiness. Ignorance of karma functions principally to cause us to continue taking lower rebirths. As long as we remain confused about actions and their effects we continue to engage in non-virtuous actions, which are the causes of such rebirths. Ignorance of emptiness functions principally to keep us bound within samsara. Even if we understand karma, until we have realized emptiness directly we continue to create the causes for cyclic rebirths.

DELUDED DOUBT

Doubt is a mental factor that engages its object two-pointedly or wavers in hesitation between two alternative viewpoints. Not all doubt is deluded doubt. Deluded doubt is a specific type of doubt where the object is anything that it is important to realize in order to attain liberation, such as karma or true sufferings, and where the hesitation is in favour of the incorrect view denying the existence of such an object. In other words, deluded doubt is a doubt that interferes with attaining liberation. The doubts we have about objects that are not important to know in order to attain liberation are not deluded. For example, if someone comes in the door and we wonder 'Is this John?', our doubt is not deluded doubt.

It is important to distinguish between deluded doubts and doubts that are the beginning of wisdom. The former are to be abandoned but the latter are necessary if we are to gain realizations. When we first listen to or read Dharma we have many doubts because Dharma contradicts our wrong views and incorrect assumptions and makes us undecided about them. This kind of indecision is a sign that we are beginning to develop wisdom, because it is the starting-point for the development of correct views. If we never develop this kind of doubt there is no way to gain conviction in Dharma teachings. For example, when we first hear teachings on emptiness we may begin to doubt 'I think that objects exist externally, but do they really?', or 'Objects seem to be substantial, but could they in fact be insubstantial, like dreams?' Without such doubts at the beginning, it is impossible to realize emptiness later. These doubts are doubts tending towards the truth. They take us in the right direction and actually help us to increase our understanding and clarity of mind.

By contrast, deluded doubts destroy our faith in what is virtuous and worthwhile and make us undecided about objects that are trustworthy and beneficial. They destroy the lucidity and joy that we experience when we generate admiring faith. They undermine our virtuous aspirations, and make our previously peaceful mind unsettled and uneasy. If we listen to or read correct Dharma instructions and think to ourself 'These teachings are probably wrong', or 'This advice is probably of no value', these are deluded doubts. If we receive correct explanations of emptiness and develop a slight understanding, and then someone comes along and argues very cleverly against the correct view so that we start to think 'The reasonings I heard before are probably wrong', this is deluded doubt. Again, if we receive from our Spiritual Guide perfect instructions for meditation but someone else, with the air of a great meditator, tells us 'That method is inferior. I know much better ways of meditating', we may doubt our Spiritual Guide and the instructions he or she has given. Such doubt can arise when we are about to perform a virtuous action or when we have embarked upon some altruistic deed. It makes us think that we have been misguided and so it destroys our good intention.

Deluded doubt is very dangerous because it quickly halts our spiritual practice and throws us into confusion. It can arise when our faith and effort degenerate, or when we hear or read something that undermines our daily practice. Deluded doubt can also arise as a result of inappropriate, excessive, or untimely analysis. There are times when it is appropriate and beneficial to apply analytical investigation, such as when we are studying subtle topics like subtle impermanence or emptiness; and there are times when it is better to refrain from analysis, such as when we have gained an adequate understanding of certain gross conventional truths. Overanalysis or untimely analysis induces excessive doubts, which interfere with our practice.

It is especially important to avoid deluded doubt when we are practising Secret Mantra because success in Tantric practices depends upon our having perfectly pure faith. If we develop deluded doubts about our practice of Secret Mantra we shall not gain much benefit, even if we practise for aeons. Therefore in Secret Mantra even blind faith is better than overanalysis because blind faith can induce strong virtuous determinations whereas overanalysis brings doubt and confusion.

DELUDED VIEW

Holding deluded views is the sixth and last of the root delusions. There are many types of deluded view but the principal is grasping at our self, or I, as inherently, or truly, existent. This view conceives the I as something that has no relationship with either the mind or the body. For example, in a situation where we are afraid or embarrassed we do not think that our mind is afraid or embarrassed, or that our body is afraid or embarrassed, but rather, 'I am afraid, I am embarrassed.' The I that we hold onto at such times is unrelated to and independent of our mind, our body, or the combination of them both. Although it is easier to see this mind at work in extreme situations, it is functioning all the time, even while we are asleep. This mistaken way of looking at our self is the chain that binds us to samsara; if this view is abandoned, all our delusions will be cut.

The deluded view of believing self and other phenomena to be independent or inherently existent is the source from which all other delusions such as anger, attachment, and pride arise. These delusions in turn impel us to create karma, and through the force of this karma we are born again and again in samsara, where we experience the relentless sufferings of birth, hunger, thirst, sickness, old age, and eventually death. All these sufferings have their source in our deluded view that conceives phenomena as inherently existent. If we want to be free from suffering we must meditate daily on the faults of holding this view.

As Bodhisattva Shantideva says, delusions are our worst enemy, keeping us trapped in the prison of samsara. What impels us to sell our time, our energy, our sweat, and indeed our very life for the sake of a little money, a few possessions, and the bubble of reputation? We are enslaved in this way by our delusions, primarily our attachment. Only our delusions have the power to harm us in so many ways.

Ordinary enemies harm us externally, but the enemy of the delusions harms us from within. Since beginningless time it has dwelt within our mind, harming us at its pleasure. This enemy is so mixed with our mind that it is very difficult to identify it and to distinguish it from virtue. Only by studying and investigating this enemy can we recognize it for what it is. There is no other method.

We say a doctor is skilful if he or she is able to identify and diagnose diseases of the body, but it requires far more skill to distinguish a non-virtuous mind from a virtuous one. How can we make such a subtle diagnosis? We need first to study Buddha's teachings, especially those on the mind, and then to use analytical meditation to apply this understanding to our own mind. In this way we can become the doctor of our own mind, identifying the various diseases of the delusions and eradicating them with the medicine of Dharma.

In Tibet there was once a very famous practitioner called Geshe Ben Gungyal. Noticing that he never recited prayers and did not appear to sleep at night, his disciples asked him what his spiritual practice was. Ben Gungyal replied: 'I have two practices – to know when delusions are arising in my mind and to control them. Other than this I have no practice. If I see that delusions are not arising I am happy, but if they do arise I watch them with mindfulness and apply the appropriate opponents. My Dharma practice is not from my mouth; my practice is to eradicate delusions.' Ben Gungyal's method of practice was greatly praised by eminent Teachers of his day, and it would be wise for us to emulate him.

We may understand how delusions harm us, but wonder if it is possible to eliminate them completely. The root of all delusions is self-grasping. If the root of a tree is cut, its trunk, branches, leaves, and fruit will wither and die. In the same way, if we cut our self-grasping with the sword of wisdom – the realization of emptiness – all of our delusions will cease forever because they originate in self-grasping. If we understand how to abandon self-grasping we shall easily eradicate all delusions from our mind.

Until we have eradicated our delusions we need to avoid falling under their influence. To do this we must guard our mind and prevent it from wandering. If we can learn to protect our mind from delusion and yoke it to the practice of virtue, our moral discipline will grow stronger until eventually it becomes perfect; but if we neglect to guard our mind many faults will arise.

A wild elephant rampaging through a village of grass huts can wreak havoc, but this is nothing compared with the damage our uncontrolled mind can inflict upon us. The wild elephant of our uncontrolled mind can bring immense suffering upon us, not just in this life but in countless future lives. If we check we can see that the creator of all the suffering of this and future lives is nothing but our own uncontrolled mind.

Many benefits follow from taming our mind. If we take the rope of mindfulness and tie our elephant mind securely to the post of virtue, all our fears will swiftly come to an end. If we wish to improve our mind and gain spiritual realizations easily, we must mix our mind with the practice of virtue by steadily applying the power of mindfulness. This is the very heart of meditation. Without mindfulness our meditations will be hollow and ineffectual, and there will be nothing to keep our wild elephant mind from roaming back and forth in its customary uncontrolled manner between objects of attachment, anger, jealousy, and so forth. We may look as if we are meditating peacefully as we sit on our meditation seat, but inside our mind is as busy as usual as we plan our next trip to the shops, visit our family and friends, or daydream of someone we feel attracted to. Just as a potter needs two hands to shape his pots, so we need the two hands of mindfulness and alertness if we are to meditate effectively and gain authentic spiritual realizations.

If we learn to control our mind through correct meditation we can overcome all our fear and anxiety. Nothing will frighten us. Why is this so? Because all fear comes from the untamed mind. A Bodhisattva who has trained his or her mind has no reason to feel afraid because he is always happy to give all his possessions and even his body to others. For us, however, it is quite different. Because we have not controlled our self-cherishing mind we immediately become anxious whenever we encounter anything even slightly threatening. The only way to overcome such fear is to tame our mind. In short, we need constantly to guard our mind with conscientiousness by relying upon mindfulness and alertness. As Bodhisattva Shantideva says:

To those who wish to guard their minds,
With folded hands I make this request –
Always strive to guard your mind
With mindfulness and alertness.

EQUANIMITY

As mentioned earlier, equanimity is a balanced mind that prevents us from developing anger and attachment by applying specific opponents. Recognizing anger and attachment to be harmful, like poison, our equanimity prevents them from developing and keeps our mind peaceful. When the mind of equanimity is manifest we are very balanced and calm because we are free from the disturbing minds of attachment, anger, and other delusions. Moreover, equanimity is the basis for developing pure love, compassion, bodhichitta, and eventually the supreme state of Buddhahood, or full enlightenment.

When we gain the realization of equanimity our mind becomes peaceful and we do not feel disturbed, even in the most difficult circumstances. This does not mean that we become callous or uncaring. Equanimity is far removed from indifference or apathy. It does not reduce our love and compassion, or our ability to rejoice in others' good fortune. Quite the opposite – it is the very foundation for increasing all these good qualities. Equanimity reduces our attachment and anger, but it does not reduce our liking and our love for others. Bodhisattvas, who have developed equanimity, have great liking for others, and they have unusually pleasant feelings towards everyone they meet. When they see someone in pain they do not feel unmoved but develop a strong wish to remove the pain, and if they can actually do this they feel overjoyed. Although Bodhisattvas have great liking for others they remain undisturbed by attachment because their minds are in the nature of love and peace. We cannot say that someone does not have equanimity just because they make friends or because they behave differently towards different people. Bodhisattvas observe the conventions of their societies. For example, in England they do not hug and kiss everyone they see just because they feel so pleasantly disposed towards them. It is impossible to tell from external behaviour whether someone has equanimity.

If we become excited or depressed when we meet other people we shall keep encountering problems, but if we can maintain a well-balanced mind our meetings with our friends will be pleasant and our friendships long-lasting. Outwardly we should try to maintain a constant and agreeable expression, one that always verges on smiling; and inwardly we should feel well-disposed towards everyone and avoid extremes of elation and depression. Someone who has a constant, warm smile and who is well-disposed to others and even-tempered, not exuberant one day then miserable the next, is like gold whose colour remains stable without varying from day to day.

Once we have developed equanimity towards all other living beings it will be very easy to maintain equanimity with regard to inanimate objects such as our living conditions, driving conditions, and the weather.

NON-HARMFULNESS

According to Asanga's *Compendium of Abhidharma*, non-harmfulness is not simply not harming others, but compassion – a mind motivated by cherishing others that sincerely wishes to release them from their suffering.

We must be careful to distinguish compassion from desirous attachment. Compassion is necessarily a virtuous mind whereas attachment is never virtuous. Sometimes our wish to help others arises principally from attachment. For example, a rider may wish his injured horse to recover so that he will not have to miss a riding event. At other times our concern for others is a mixture of attachment and compassion. This is often the case when we wish for our friends or relatives to be free from suffering. Pure compassion, however, is completely free from attachment and is exclusively concerned with the welfare of others.

When we have compassion our disturbing minds such as pride, jealousy, anger, and attachment are naturally pacified and our mind becomes very peaceful. Our compassion also makes others happy because we naturally care for others and try to help them whenever we can.

Buddha said:

You are your own protector,
You are your own enemy.

If we have deep compassion and wisdom we can protect ourself from suffering and danger, and so become our own protector; but if we allow anger and ignorance to destroy our happiness and good fortune we are harming ourself, and so become our own enemy. Whether we are our own protector or our own enemy is our choice, our responsibility.

Some people believe that only humans experiencing manifest suffering are worthy objects of compassion, implying that animals and humans experiencing relative comfort are not. This is wrong. Animals and insects have minds, and, like humans, experience pleasure and pain. However, although they are the same as humans in that they seek to experience happiness and avoid suffering, in reality they experience far greater suffering than humans. Animals have no freedom; without choice they are exploited by humans for entertainment, experimentation, and food, with no regard for their feelings. If we think carefully about this we shall realize that it is very necessary to cultivate compassion for animals, and instead of abusing them or taking their lives we should help and protect them.

Similarly, other humans who enjoy a good life, as well as those who dislike us, and even those we do not know, should be objects of our compassion. In reality everyone without exception has to experience the sufferings of attachment, anger, jealousy, and ignorance. No ordinary being, whether animal or human, rich or poor, has permanent liberation from suffering. They all have to experience the cycle of uncontrolled death and rebirth in life after life, and so they are all suitable objects of our compassion.

The main function of non-harmfulness, or compassion, is to prevent us from harming others. A person whose mind is filled with compassion can never wish to hurt anyone. It is only because we lack compassion that we sometimes develop the intention to hurt others. Compassion and harmful intentions are like water and fire – completely incompatible. Refraining from harming others is one of the most important practices for a Buddhist. If we always practise non-harmfulness we shall always be practising Buddha's teachings, even if we cannot do formal meditation.

Buddha said that we should cultivate compassion for all living beings without discrimination and dedicate all our actions to their benefit and happiness. If we take this advice to heart and put it into practice we shall become a realized being, like a Bodhisattva, and our way of life will become like the Bodhisattva's way of life. In this way we shall definitely attain the eternal happiness of full enlightenment.

To cultivate compassion for all living beings we need to train our mind in a special way. We contemplate:

I am only one whereas others are countless. My happiness and suffering are insignificant when compared with the happiness and suffering of all other living beings.

If we really feel that the happiness of others is important we shall find it easy to generate a genuine wish to release them all from their suffering. This sincere wish is compassion. We meditate on it for as long as possible.

This is a simple method for cultivating compassion for all living beings, but success in this depends upon first developing a mind that cherishes all living beings. Detailed advice on how to cherish others can be found in *Eight Steps to Happiness*.

Because we are beings of the desire realm, most of our problems arise from attachment. If we check carefully we shall find that even war is mainly caused by attachment. We have such strong attachment to our happiness, views, wishes, possessions, and so forth that if our wishes are not fulfilled we easily become angry, and this can lead to fighting and even to killing. Compassion opposes attachment. Whereas attachment arises from inappropriate attention, compassion arises from appropriate attention; and attachment and compassion can never manifest at the same time. Therefore, if we have compassion there will be no basis for arguments or harming others.

Great compassion is born of renunciation. If we can understand our own samsara and develop renunciation for it, we can understand the samsara of others and develop compassion for them. As humans we each experience a great deal of suffering and so it is relatively easy for us to see the faults of samsara and develop a wish to be free from it. If we then turn our attention to others we shall see that they too are experiencing immense suffering, and develop compassion for them.

Compassion is a powerful way to purify our mind. If our mind is pure, the objects of our mind are also pure. We shall experience everything – our environment, enjoyments, body, and mind – as pure. With a pure mind we can see holy beings such as Buddhas and Bodhisattvas directly. This is a very important subject, but one that is not easy to understand at first. To begin with we need to understand the relationship between an object and the mind that apprehends it. Normally we believe that the object exists 'out there', independent of our mind, while the mind is 'in here'. We therefore experience a gap between our mind and its object, and this indicates that in reality we do not understand the relationship between them. Take for example our mind perceiving this book. We perceive the book as completely independent of the mind, and as having no relationship with the mind – our mind is here and the book is there. This is a mistaken appearance.

Buddha's wisdom teachings explain that phenomena do not exist from their own side. However, it can be difficult to understand what this means. It is not enough to say it verbally; we need to gain a deep understanding of its true meaning. Our body has no independent existence; it does not exist from its own side, independently of the mind. How then does it exist? To understand this we need to study books such as *The Meditation Handbook* and *Heart of Wisdom*, which explain the emptiness of the self, the body, and other phenomena. We should try to understand how things do not exist from their own side but exist as mere imputations of the mind, as mere appearances to the mind like objects in a dream.

In this way we shall understand how objects depend upon the subjective mind. These mere appearances are manifestations of emptiness and have no independent existence. They do not exist from their own side. Thus, whether an object is pure or impure, beautiful or ugly, pleasant or unpleasant, depends upon the mind. If the mind is pure,

140

its object is pure; but for as long as our mind remains impure we shall experience only impure objects.

There are many accounts of spiritual practitioners who by developing strong compassion purified their minds of the negativity that had long been obstructing their spiritual progress. For example, the Indian Buddhist Master Arya Asanga longed to see the enlightened being Buddha Maitreya directly. To achieve this he entered a retreat on the yoga of Buddha Maitreya, but after three years of meditation he had still not received a vision. Discouraged, he abandoned his retreat and left the cave. As he was walking down the mountain he met an old man repeatedly stroking a huge iron block with a feather. Asanga asked him what he was doing, and the man replied 'I am cutting this iron block.' When Asanga asked 'How is it possible to cut an iron block with a feather?', the old man, who in reality was an emanation of Maitreya, replied: 'Look, I have already made some progress. If I continue patiently I can definitely complete what I have set out to do.' Asanga thought to himself: 'This man is putting great effort into achieving such an insignificant goal! Surely if I continue patiently with my retreat I can complete my goal and bring real benefit to the people of this world.' Thus encouraged, he returned to his cave.

After another three years Asanga had still not received a vision of Maitreya. Again he became discouraged and decided to abandon his retreat. On his way home he passed by a waterfall and noticed a trickle of water that, by continuously dripping onto the rock below, had carved out a smooth channel. He thought: 'These tiny drops of water have worn away hard rock through their persistence. Surely if I am equally persistent in my meditation I can wear away the hard rock of my inner obstructions and accomplish my goal.' With this thought he once again returned to his cave.

After another three years' retreat, still with no success, he again became discouraged and left his cave. This time he saw a hole in a cliff face inside which some birds had made their nests. He noticed that as the birds flew in and out the tips of their wings brushed against the rock, and over the years had worn a niche into it. Inspired by this example of how even the gentlest action if repeated often enough can produce dramatic results, he returned to his cave determined to remove the obstructions from his mind.

After meditating for another three years, Asanga had completed twelve years of retreat. However, not realizing that he was now close to receiving a vision, he decided disappointedly to return home. On his way down from the cave he came across an old dog lying in the middle of the path. Its body was covered in maggot-infested sores, and it seemed close to death. Overwhelmed by compassion, Asanga decided to remove the maggots. Realizing that if he picked them up with his fingers he would hurt them, he decided to remove them very gently with his tongue. Again he developed compassion, thinking that if he put the maggots on the ground they would die of starvation. He therefore cut off part of his thigh, but just as he was pain-stakingly transferring the maggots with his tongue onto the piece of his own flesh the dying dog suddenly disap-peared and Maitreya appeared in front of him. Once Asanga had recovered from his surprise he asked Maitreya 'Why did I have to wait so long to see you?' Maitreya replied 'I have been with you since the very beginning of your retreat, but because of your karmic obstructions you were unable to see me.' Through having generated great compassion Asanga had purified his mind and finally received the vision he had longed for.

There is a story about Khädrubje, one of Je Tsongkhapa's heart disciples, that also illustrates the power of compas-sion to purify the mind and enable us to see holy beings directly. One day, after Je Tsongkhapa had passed away, Khädrubje was contemplating how the minds of sentient beings in these degenerate times were so rough – polluted by strong delusions and wrong views. 'How can I help all these poor mother beings?' he thought, and tears of compassion fell from his eyes. As a result of Khädrubje's compassion, Je Tsongkhapa appeared directly in front of him and asked 'My Son, what is the problem? Why are you crying?' When Khädrubje told him of his desire to alleviate the suffering of all sentient beings, Je Tsongkhapa encouraged him, saying: 'Don't worry. Be patient and confident, and I will help you.'

Compassion is also a powerful cause of taking rebirth in a Pure Land. Anyone who dies with a mind of pure compassion will definitely take his or her next rebirth in a Pure Land. Geshe Chekhawa, author of *Training the Mind in Seven Points*, made universal compassion his daily practice. He had the realization of exchanging self with others, and told his disciples that his main wish was to take rebirth in hell so that he could help the beings there. However, when he was dying he perceived a vision of the Pure Land, and told his disciples 'I have not fulfilled my wish; I have to go to the Pure Land!' Because the sun of his compassion had dispelled the darkness of impure appearance, he had no choice but to go to the Pure Land. More about the life and teachings of Geshe Chekhawa can be found in *Universal Compassion*.

Once in Tibet a man fell into a river and was being carried away by the current. An onlooker on the bank saw that he could not swim and was in danger of drowning, and, with a compassionate wish to save him, spontaneously jumped into the river. However, like most Tibetans he too could not swim, and so both men drowned. A Yogi living in the area saw with his clairvoyance that the man who had tried to save the other was reborn in a Pure Land. Why? Because he died with a mind of compassion. Compassion purifies our mind and transforms our actions into pure actions, and pure actions produce pure results.

Compassion has countless good qualities. For example, many people want to become qualified doctors to help cure disease; but the best method to become a qualified doctor is to develop compassion. If a doctor has compassion for all living beings, his or her patients receive Buddha's blessings through that doctor, and so he is able to cure the disease more easily. Therefore whatever the doctor does, whether it be conducting an examination, giving an injection, operating, or administering medicine, the patients will receive Buddha's blessings through him.

Of course, because most diseases are physical and our bodies are physical forms, a cure sometimes depends upon external conditions such as the correct medicine. However, even if the doctor is unable to cure the disease, if he or she has universal compassion his patients will still gain immense benefit through receiving Buddha's blessings. They will feel happy and positive and receive many virtuous imprints. Their negative minds will cease and their mental peace will increase. Through this we can understand that anyone who wishes to become a qualified doctor should strive to develop universal compassion. We can say that the actions of a compassionate doctor and the actions of Buddha are similar because they both have compassion for all living beings. Such a doctor is like Medicine Buddha.

If we want to cure others' mental and physical problems we need to put great effort into developing universal compassion. We cannot really heal the suffering of others for as long as we have self-cherishing; an ordinary being cannot heal another ordinary being. A qualified healer must develop the internal realization of compassion.

Similarly, many people want to become spiritual Teachers to benefit others, but again the best method to become a qualified Teacher is to develop universal compassion. Like a doctor, if a Teacher has compassion for all living beings, whenever he or she is giving teachings and helping others people will receive Buddha's blessings through that Teacher. His or her teachings will become powerful medicine to cure the diseases of the delusions. Such a Teacher is fully qualified to lead living beings to the bliss of liberation and full enlightenment.

It is said that because all living beings have some compassion, all living beings have Buddha nature. By gradually
improving and extending our compassion we shall eventually develop great, or universal, compassion – the wish to
protect all living beings from suffering. From the moment
we develop compassion for all living beings our Buddha
nature awakens and begins to function. Thus through the
force of our compassion we can enter the Mahayana path
and progress through all the stages to enlightenment. If we
then improve our great compassion it will eventually transform into the compassion of a Buddha, which has the power
actually to protect all living beings. A Buddha's compassion
can appear as any object that living beings may need, such
as specific environments, enjoyments, friends, spiritual
Teachers, doctors, or medicines. Compassion helps everyone – it pervades everywhere.

Contemplating all these benefits of universal compassion,
we make a strong determination to cultivate and maintain
compassion for all living beings without exception. We
meditate on this determination and then put it into practice
in our daily life.

Having generated compassion for living beings, sincerely
wanting to help them all without exception, we shall realize
that right now we lack the ability to do this, and that it is
only enlightened beings who have such power. Motivated by
our compassion we shall then develop the mind of bodhichitta, wishing to attain enlightenment for the benefit of
all. To fulfil the two intentions of bodhichitta – to release all
living beings from samsaric rebirth and to attain the great
liberation of a Buddha – we can take the Bodhisattva vows
and transform all our daily activities into the Bodhisattva's
way of life. Gradually, by completing the Bodhisattva's path
– the realizations of the six perfections – we can attain the
great liberation of a Buddha, full enlightenment.

Buddha King of Mount Meru

Purification and Prayer

THE FORCE OF DESTRUCTION

In this context 'destruction' refers to the purification practice that destroys or purifies our accumulated non-virtue. The ripened effect of non-virtue is lower rebirth, so without purifying our negative karma it will be very difficult for us to take a higher rebirth in the future. It is especially important for powa practitioners to purify their negative karma because this is the main obstacle to their taking rebirth in the Pure Land of a Buddha.

If we find this difficult to believe we can consider the following. In samsara there are countless beings in the lower realms, such as animals and hell beings, and countless beings in the higher realms, such as humans and gods. Even among humans some are born in wealthy countries among happy families where life is easy and pleasant, while others are born in poor countries, experiencing great poverty and many difficulties. All these different rebirths are taken without choice – no one ordered: 'You should take a higher rebirth, you should take a lower one; you should go to a rich country, you to a poor one.' No one would ever choose to be born as an animal, an insect, or a human being who is poor, sick, or destitute. So the question is, why do some beings take higher rebirth and others lower rebirth? Why are some people born into rich families, while others are born into poverty? Unless we follow Buddha's teachings it is not possible to find a correct answer. Through his omniscient wisdom Buddha explained the subtle connection between actions, or karma, and their effects. Buddhas know that non-virtuous actions are the main cause of taking a lower rebirth, and virtuous actions are the main cause of taking a higher rebirth. Human rebirth itself is the effect of virtue, but human suffering is the effect of non-virtue. Poverty, for example, results from a previous negative action of stealing.

If we carefully study Buddha's teachings on karma we cannot avoid the conclusion that living beings have different experiences because they accumulate different karma. According to Buddha's teachings, all happiness and suffering are created by mind because all actions are motivated by the mental factor intention. For example, although no one wants to experience suffering, many people like to kill other living beings for their enjoyment; and thus without realizing that killing is a non-virtuous action they unwittingly create the causes of their own future suffering.

We have already accumulated infinite non-virtuous actions earlier in this life and in our countless previous lives, and if we do not purify these they will definitely throw us into a lower rebirth where it will be impossible for us to engage in spiritual practice. Even now these non-virtuous actions and broken spiritual commitments are seriously obstructing the fulfilment of our wishes and our spiritual progress. It is vital that we purify them without delay. The ability to purify our non-virtuous actions is one of the main advantages of a human rebirth. Animals have very little capacity to engage in virtuous actions, and naturally perform many negative actions such as killing; but human beings have the freedom not only to refrain from non-virtue but also to purify the potentialities of all their previously accumulated negative karma. As the Kadampa Geshes used to say: 'Now is the time to purify negative karma, not to create more! Now is the time to accumulate merit, not to use it up!' If we lose this precious human life it will be almost impossible to find another such opportunity.

The actual practice of purification is explained in four parts:

1 The power of regret
2 The power of reliance
3 The power of the opponent force
4 The power of promise

These are known as the 'four opponent powers' because they have the power to purify completely all the non-virtue we have accumulated since beginningless time. Every non-virtuous action gives rise to four different effects: the ripened effect, the effect that is an experience similar to the cause, the effect that is a tendency similar to the cause, and the environmental effect. The action of killing, for example, has as its ripened effect rebirth in any of the three lower realms – the animal realm, the hungry spirit realm, or the hell realm. The experience similar to the cause of killing is that in subsequent rebirths we suffer from physical pain, poor health, and a short life. The tendency similar to the cause of killing is that in life after life we have a strong propensity to kill living beings. This is the worst effect because it traps us in a vicious cycle of killing. Finally, the environmental effect of killing is that the place in which we live is impure, making it hard to find uncontaminated food, air, water, and so forth, which in turn causes us to suffer from ill health.

The power of regret purifies the potential for the effect that is an experience similar to the cause; the power of reliance purifies the potential for the environmental effect; the power of the opponent force purifies the potential for the ripened effect; and the power of promise purifies the potential for the effect that is a tendency similar to the cause. By engaging in sincere purification using the four opponent powers we can destroy the potentialities for the four effects of all non-virtuous actions, thereby attaining permanent freedom from mental and physical suffering, and especially from rebirth in the three lower realms. In this way we can take the real essence of our precious human life. How wonderful!

The way to practise purification using the four opponent powers will now be explained based on the *Mahayana Confession Sutra*, also known as the *Sutra of the Three Superior Heaps* and *The Bodhisattva's Confession of Moral Downfalls*, which can be found in Appendix II. This is explained in detail in *The Bodhisattva Vow*.

THE POWER OF REGRET

If we swallowed even the tiniest drop of poison we would be terrified of its imminent effect, but our fear of the effects of our past negative actions should be far greater. External poison may cause us to become sick or even to die, but it can harm us only in this life. The internal poison of our negative karma, on the other hand, harms us in all our lives, causing endless physical and mental pain, and preventing us from attaining higher rebirth and spiritual realizations. Since this poison is already within our mental continuum we must develop strong regret and make a determination to purify the potentials of our negative actions as quickly as possible. Having meditated on this determination we then put it into practice.

THE POWER OF RELIANCE

Through sincerely relying upon the Three Jewels we can completely purify all our non-virtuous actions and accomplish the ultimate refuge of Buddhahood. Therefore we need to go for refuge by sincerely relying upon Buddha, Dharma, and Sangha. This is the meaning of the power of reliance.

We first visualize the objects of refuge to whom we make confession. In the space in front of us we visualize Buddha Shakyamuni seated on a throne, on cushions of a lotus, moon, and sun. His body is the colour of gold and he is in the posture known as 'Buddha Shakyamuni Conquering the Maras'. His legs are in the vajra posture. His right arm is held with the elbow at the hip and the forearm on the right thigh extending to his knee so that his middle finger touches the sun cushion. This mudra indicates that he has conquered the Devaputra mara. His left hand rests palm upwards below his navel in the mudra of meditative equipoise, and holds a precious bowl made of lapis lazuli containing three nectars indicating that he has conquered the mara of uncontrolled death, the mara of contaminated aggregates, and the mara of the delusions. He wears the three robes of an ordained person, and his body is adorned with the thirty-two signs and eighty indications of a Buddha. His body is the synthesis of all Sangha Jewels, his speech the synthesis of all Dharma Jewels, and his mind the synthesis of all Buddha Jewels.

He is surrounded by the other thirty-four Confession Buddhas. We firmly believe that these enlightened beings are actually present in the space in front of us, and with strong faith in the Three Jewels we contemplate:

By relying upon Buddha, Dharma, and Sangha I will purify all my non-virtuous actions and accomplish the Buddha Jewel so that I can benefit all living beings without exception.

We meditate on this intention for a short while.

THE POWER OF THE OPPONENT FORCE

Whereas the other three opponent powers are like limbs supporting a body, the power of the opponent force is like the body itself because it is the direct opponent to all the negative effects of our non-virtuous actions.

To practise the power of the opponent force we visualize the potentials of all our negative karma in the form of a dark mass at our heart, and we strongly believe that the Thirty-five Confession Buddhas have the power to purify all this negative karma. Remembering the specific function of each Buddha to purify particular non-virtues, as explained in

The Bodhisattva Vow, with the powers of regret and reliance we make prostrations to the holy beings, and request them to purify our non-virtues and broken commitments, while reciting the *Mahayana Confession Sutra* and concentrating on its meaning. Because this practice is done in conjunction with prostrations it is especially powerful.

As a result of making these requests we imagine that wisdom lights and nectars flow from the hearts of the holy beings, enter our body through our crown, reach our heart, and completely destroy the mass of darkness – the potentials of all our negative karma – just as the light of the sun destroys the darkness of night. Firmly believing that we have actually purified our negative karma, we generate a feeling of joy and maintain this feeling single-pointedly.

THE POWER OF PROMISE

The definition of non-virtuous action is any action of body, speech, or mind that is the main cause of suffering. Since we wish to avoid suffering we must stop creating its causes. With this thought we first develop and then maintain the intention to refrain from all non-virtuous actions of body, speech, and mind.

The power of promise has many different levels, according to our capacity. At the beginning we can only develop the intention to refrain from all negative actions. We then need to strengthen this intention until it becomes stable, at which point we can make the actual promise to refrain from all negative actions.

To generate the power of promise we contemplate how every non-virtuous action gives rise to the four types of effect, as explained above and, in more detail, in *Joyful Path of Good Fortune*. In this way we shall develop deep regret for all the negative actions we have committed in the past, and a strong determination to refrain from committing them in the future will arise naturally.

In summary, to purify our non-virtues we first develop strong regret for having created them by remembering that they are the main cause of all our present and future suffering. We then apply the power of reliance by thinking:

Since only Buddha, Dharma, and Sangha have the power to protect living beings from suffering and its causes, I must rely upon them from the depths of my heart, and through receiving their blessings completely purify all my non-virtues.

Having generated this motivation we then practise the power of the opponent force, in this case making prostrations to the Thirty-five Confession Buddhas. At the end of each session we make a promise, or at least generate the intention, to refrain from all non-virtuous actions in the future.

THE FORCE OF ASPIRATIONAL PRAYER

With this precious human life we have a great opportunity to accomplish two important things: (1) the realizations of the stages of the path, from the realization of relying upon the Spiritual Guide to the realization of superior seeing, and (2) the Pure Land of a Buddha. These two accomplishments are the very essence of our human life.

The essential method for fulfilling both these aims has been explained in this book; now we need to make prayers in order to achieve our goals. As mentioned above, if with strong faith and conviction we dedicate our virtues to a specific goal, we shall definitely achieve that goal; so if we dedicate our virtues to accomplishing the realizations of the stages of the path and the Pure Land of a Buddha, we shall definitely meet with success. Making special prayers for the success of our practice is the force of aspirational prayer.

We begin any practice of the stages of the path by making special prayers to attain the realization of that practice, and we finish by dedicating the merit we have accumulated to the realization of that practice. For example, if we are going to meditate on powa we make repeated requests to all the enlightened beings to grant us their blessings so that we may attain this specific realization; and after the meditation we dedicate our merit to our attainment of this realization by reciting the appropriate verse from the following prayer.

We can use this prayer as dedication verses for all the other meditations of the stages of the path. In general it is very important to dedicate all our virtuous actions – such as making offerings and practising giving, moral discipline, patience, effort, concentration, and wisdom – to our attainment of all the stages of the path to enlightenment and the Pure Land of a Buddha. To do this we can chant or recite the following prayer while concentrating on its meaning:

Realizing that the path begins with strong reliance
On my Spiritual Guide, the holy, supreme Field of
Merit,
Through the force of our virtuous actions such as
making offerings and prostrations
May I and all mother beings gain the realization of
relying upon the Spiritual Guide.

Realizing that this precious human life, found only
once,
Is difficult to attain, and yet decays so quickly,
May I seize its essential meaning,
Undistracted by the meaningless activities of this
life.

Fearing the blazing fires of the sufferings of lower
realms ˙
From the depths of my heart I go for refuge to
Buddha, Dharma, and Sangha.
May I strive sincerely
To abandon non-virtue and practise the entire
collection of virtue.

Being violently tossed by the waves of delusion
and karma
And tormented by the sea monsters of the three
sufferings,
May I develop a strong wish for liberation
From the boundless and fearful great ocean of
samsara.

Forsaking the mind that views as a pleasure garden
This unbearable prison of samsara,
May I take up the victory banner of liberation
By maintaining the three higher trainings and the
wealths of Superiors.

Contemplating how all these pitiful migrators are
my mothers,
Who out of kindness have cherished me again and
again,
May I generate a spontaneous compassion
Like that of a loving mother for her dearest child.

In that no one wishes for even the slightest
suffering,
Or is ever content with the happiness they have,
There is no difference between myself and others;
Realizing this, may I joyfully make others happy.

Seeing that this chronic disease of cherishing myself
Is the cause that gives rise to unwanted suffering,
May I destroy this great demon of selfishness
By resenting it as the object of blame.

Seeing that the mind that cherishes mother beings
and would secure their happiness
Is the gateway that leads to infinite good qualities,
May I cherish these beings more than my life,
Even if they rise up against me as my enemies.

In short, since the childish are concerned for
    themselves alone,
Whereas Buddhas work solely for the sake of others,
May I distinguish the faults and benefits,
And thus be able to exchange myself with others.

Since cherishing myself is the door to all faults
And cherishing mother beings is the foundation of
    all good qualities,
May I take as my essential practice
The yoga of exchanging self with others.

Therefore, O Compassionate, Venerable Spiritual
    Guide,
May all the suffering, negativities, and obstructions
    of mother sentient beings
Ripen upon me right now;
And through my giving my happiness and virtue to
    others,
May all migrating beings be happy.

Though the world and its beings, filled with the
    effects of evil,
Pour down unwanted suffering like rain,
This is a chance to exhaust the effects of negative
    actions;
Seeing this, may I transform adverse conditions
    into the path.

In short, whether favourable or unfavourable
    conditions arise,
May I transform them into the path of improving
    the two bodhichittas
Through practising the five forces, the essence of
    all Dharmas,
And thereby maintain a happy mind alone.

May I make this precious human life extremely
 meaningful
By immediately applying meditation to whatever
 I meet
Through the skilful means of the four preparations,
And by practising the commitments and precepts of
 training the mind.

Through love, compassion, and superior intention,
And the magical practice of mounting taking and
 giving upon the breath,
May I generate the actual bodhichitta,
To free all migrators from this great ocean of
 samsara.

May I strive sincerely on the sole path
Traversed by all the Conquerors of the three times –
To bind my mind with pure Bodhisattva vows
And practise the three moral disciplines of the
 Mahayana.

May I complete the perfection of giving
Through the instructions on improving the mind of
 giving without attachment,
And thus transform my body, my enjoyments, and
 my virtues amassed throughout the three times
Into whatever each sentient being desires.

May I complete the perfection of moral discipline
By not transgressing even at the cost of my life
The discipline of the Pratimoksha, Bodhisattva, and
 Secret Mantra vows,
And by gathering virtuous Dharmas, and
 accomplishing the welfare of sentient beings.

May I complete the perfection of patience
So that even if every single being in the three
  realms,
Out of anger were to abuse me, criticize me,
  threaten me, or even take my life,
Undisturbed, I would repay their harm by helping
  them.

May I complete the perfection of effort
By striving for supreme enlightenment with
  unwavering compassion;
Even if I must remain in the fires of the deepest
  hell
For many aeons for the sake of each being.

May I complete the perfection of concentration
By abandoning the faults of mental sinking, mental
  excitement, and mental wandering,
And concentrating in single-pointed absorption
On the state that is the lack of true existence of all
  phenomena.

May I complete the perfection of wisdom
Through the yoga of the space-like meditative
  equipoise on the ultimate,
With the great bliss of the suppleness
Induced by the wisdom of individual analysis of
  thatness.

Outer and inner phenomena are like illusions, like
  dreams,
And like reflections of the moon in a clear lake,
For though they appear they do not truly exist;
Realizing this, may I complete the illusion-like
  concentration.

May I realize the meaning of Nagarjuna's intention,
That there is no contradiction but only harmony
Between the absence of even an atom of inherent
    existence in samsara and nirvana
And the non-deceptive dependent relationship of
    cause and effect.

And then the swirling ocean of the Tantras is
    crossed
Through the kindness of the navigator, the Vajra
    Holder.
May I cherish more than my life
The vows and commitments, the root of attainments.

Through the yoga of the first stage that transforms
    birth, death, and bardo,
Into the three bodies of the Conquerors,
May I purify all stains of ordinary appearance and
    conception,
And see whatever appears as the form of the Deity.

O Protector, please place your feet
On the centre of the eight-petalled lotus at my heart,
So that I may manifest within this life
The paths of illusory body, clear light, and union.

If by the time of my death I have not completed the
    path,
May I attain the Pure Land of Buddha
Through the instruction on correctly applying the
    five forces,
The supremely powerful method of transference to
    Buddhahood.   (3x)

In short, O Supreme Spiritual Guide, throughout
all my lives
May I never be separated from you, but always
come under your care;
And as the foremost of your disciples,
Maintain all the secrets of your body, speech, and
mind.

O Supreme Spiritual Guide, wherever you manifest
as a Buddha,
May I be the very first in your retinue;
And may everything be auspicious for me to
accomplish without effort
All temporary and ultimate needs and wishes.

Due to my making requests in this way, O Supreme
Spiritual Guide,
With delight, please come to my crown to bestow
your blessings;
And once again firmly place your radiant feet
On the anthers of the lotus at my heart.

Appendix I
The Condensed Meaning
of the Text

———

The Condensed Meaning
of the Text

The explanation of the practice of powa has two parts:

1 Practising powa to benefit ourself and others
2 Integrating the five forces into the practice of powa

Practising powa to benefit ourself and others has four parts:

1 Engaging in the preliminary practices
2 Training in the actual powa meditation
3 Applying the practice of powa at the time of death
4 Applying the practice of powa for the benefit of others

Engaging in the preliminary practices has two parts:

1 The practice during the meditation session
2 The practice during the meditation break

The practice during the meditation session has seven parts:

1 Going for refuge and generating bodhichitta
2 Visualizing Arya Avalokiteshvara
3 Prayer of seven limbs
4 Offering the mandala
5 Requesting the five great meanings
6 Mantra recitation
7 The three recognitions

Prayer of seven limbs has seven parts:

1 Prostration
2 Offering
3 Confession
4 Rejoicing
5 Beseeching the holy beings to remain
6 Requesting the turning of the Wheel of Dharma
7 Dedication

Training in the actual powa meditation has six parts:

1 Visualization
2 The three awarenesses
3 Short mandala offering
4 Requests
5 The actual meditation
6 Dedication

Applying the practice of powa at the time of death has six parts:

1 The causes of death
2 The conditions of death
3 The signs of death
4 The minds of death
5 The sign that dying has ended
6 How to apply the practice of powa at the time of death

Applying the practice of powa for the benefit of others has two parts:

1 Understanding death, the intermediate state, and rebirth
2 How to apply the practice of powa for the benefit of others

Understanding death, the intermediate state, and rebirth has three parts:

1 Understanding death
2 Understanding the intermediate state
3 Understanding rebirth

How to apply the practice of powa for the benefit of others has two parts:

1 Benefiting the deceased
2 Benefiting those who are about to die

Benefiting the deceased has two parts:

1 Benefiting the deceased through the practice of powa
2 Benefiting the deceased by means of prayer and dedication

Benefiting the deceased through the practice of powa has two parts:

1 Self-generation
2 The actual practice

Self-generation has seven parts:

1 Going for refuge and generating bodhichitta
2 Generating the four immeasurables
3 Self-generation as Avalokiteshvara
4 Offerings to the self-generation
5 Praise
6 Mantra recitation
7 Dedication

The actual practice has three parts:

1 Generating the deceased as a living person
2 Purifying the negative karma of the deceased
3 Transferring the consciousness of the deceased to the Pure Land

Transferring the consciousness of the deceased to the Pure Land has seven parts:

1 Visualization
2 The three awarenesses
3 Prayer of seven limbs
4 Short mandala offering
5 Requests
6 The actual meditation
7 Dedication

Benefiting the deceased by means of prayer and dedication has two parts:

1 Accumulating a great collection of merit and wisdom
2 Dedicating this collection to the benefit of the deceased

Integrating the five forces into the practice of powa has five parts:

1 The force of motivation
2 The force of familiarity
3 The force of white seed
4 The force of destruction
5 The force of aspirational prayer

The force of white seed has eleven parts:

1 Faith
2 Sense of shame
3 Consideration for others
4 Non-attachment
5 Non-hatred
6 Non-ignorance
7 Effort
8 Mental suppleness
9 Conscientiousness
10 Equanimity
11 Non-harmfulness

Conscientiousness has two parts:

1 An explanation of conscientiousness
2 An explanation of the six root delusions

An explanation of the six root delusions has six parts:

1 Attachment
2 Anger
3 Deluded pride
4 Ignorance
5 Deluded doubt
6 Deluded view

The force of destruction has four parts:

1 The power of regret
2 The power of reliance
3 The power of the opponent force
4 The power of promise

Appendix II
Sadhanas

CONTENTS

Pathway to the Pure Land

————

SADHANA FOR POWA TRAINING

Introduction

In general, transference of consciousness, or powa, involves the mind leaving the body and going to a higher state through the force of meditation. Thus when we are training in powa we are learning to separate our mind from our body through meditation. Although it is sometimes said that successful powa training will gradually shorten one's life span, the training presented in this sadhana poses no such danger.

This special powa practice has the same function as Vajrayogini's uncommon yoga of inconceivability; through this training we can attain a Buddha's Pure Land such as Pure Dakini Land without abandoning this human body.

The instruction presented in this sadhana is a combination of the common powa instructions, such as those written by the first Panchen Lama and Ngulchu Dharmabhadra, and the uncommon powa instructions that come from the Ganden oral lineage. We are extremely fortunate to have the opportunity to receive and practise this profound instruction.

Pathway to the Pure Land

THE PRELIMINARY PRACTICES

Going for refuge and generating bodhichitta

I and all sentient beings, until we achieve enlightenment,
Go for refuge to Buddha, Dharma, and Sangha.
Through the virtues I collect by giving and other
    perfections,
May I become a Buddha for the benefit of all.   (3x)

Visualizing Arya Avalokiteshvara

I and all living beings as extensive as space
Have at our crowns a white lotus and a moon seat.
Upon these, from HRIH, arises Arya Avalokiteshvara.
He has a white, translucent body that radiates
    five-coloured lights.
He has a smiling expression, and gazes upon us with
    eyes of compassion.
He has four hands, the first two pressed together at his
    heart,
And the lower two holding a crystal mala and a white
    lotus flower.
He is adorned with silks and jewelled ornaments
And wears an upper garment of an antelope skin.
His crown is adorned with Amitabha.
He sits with his legs crossed in the vajra posture,
Supported from behind by a stainless moon.
He is the synthesis of all objects of refuge.

171

Prayer of seven limbs

Prostration

From every pore of my body I emanate another body,
From every pore of these bodies I emanate yet more
    bodies.
With these countless emanated bodies filling the whole
    world
I prostrate to you, Avalokiteshvara, Buddha of compassion.

Offering

The ultimate nature of all forms throughout infinite
    worlds
Appears as countless white Rupavajras pervading space.
These beautiful goddesses holding mirrors reflecting the
    whole universe
I offer to you, Avalokiteshvara, Buddha of compassion.

The ultimate nature of all sounds throughout infinite
    worlds
Appears as countless blue Shaptavajras pervading space.
These beautiful goddesses playing enchanting flutes
I offer to you, Avalokiteshvara, Buddha of compassion.

The ultimate nature of all smells throughout infinite
    worlds
Appears as countless yellow Gändhavajras pervading
    space.
These beautiful goddesses holding precious shells of
    sweet-smelling perfumes
I offer to you, Avalokiteshvara, Buddha of compassion.

The ultimate nature of all tastes throughout infinite
    worlds
Appears as countless red Rasavajras pervading space.
These beautiful goddesses holding jewelled vessels filled
    with three precious nectars
I offer to you, Avalokiteshvara, Buddha of compassion.

The ultimate nature of all touch throughout infinite
    worlds
Appears as countless green Parshavajras pervading space.
These beautiful goddesses holding heavenly garments of
    supremely soft touch
I offer to you, Avalokiteshvara, Buddha of compassion.

Confession

In the presence of the great Compassionate Ones I confess
    with a mind of great regret
All the non-virtues and negative actions that, since
    beginningless time,
I have done, ordered to be done, or rejoiced in;
And I promise that from now on I shall not commit
    them again.

Rejoicing

All Buddhas once wandered the painful paths of
    samsara, just as I do now;
But through great effort they entered the Bodhisattva's
    path
And, progressing through all its stages, attained
    complete enlightenment.
From the depths of my heart I rejoice in their virtuous
    attainments; may I become just like them.

Beseeching the holy beings to remain

Without Spiritual Guides who are manifestations of
    Buddha's compassion
Leading sentient beings on the path to liberation, this
    world would be plunged into spiritual darkness.
O Holy enlightened beings, I request you from the
    depths of my heart,
Please remain with us for countless aeons to illuminate
    the spiritual path.

Requesting the turning of the Wheel of Dharma

Through Brahma and Indra requesting Buddha to turn
the Wheel of Dharma,
Buddha taught many methods for curing the diseases of
the delusions,
Which have led countless beings to liberation from
suffering;
Therefore, I request the holy beings to teach the precious
Dharma.

Dedication

Through the virtues I have accumulated by making
prostrations, offerings, and so forth,
May holy Dharma flourish and all living beings
accomplish the stages of the path.
In particular, may I attain the Pure Land of a Buddha
And lead all living beings to the fully enlightened state.

Offering the mandala

OM VAJRA BHUMI AH HUM
Great and powerful golden ground,
OM VAJRA REKHE AH HUM
At the edge the iron fence stands around the outer circle.
In the centre Mount Meru the king of mountains,
Around which are four continents:
In the east, Purvavideha, in the south, Jambudipa,
In the west, Aparagodaniya, in the north, Uttarakuru.
Each has two sub-continents:
Deha and Videha, Tsamara and Abatsamara,
Satha and Uttaramantrina, Kurava and Kaurava.
The mountain of jewels, the wish-granting tree,
The wish-granting cow, and the harvest unsown.
The precious wheel, the precious jewel,
The precious queen, the precious minister,

The precious elephant, the precious supreme horse,
The precious general, and the great treasure vase.
The goddess of beauty, the goddess of garlands,
The goddess of music, the goddess of dance,
The goddess of flowers, the goddess of incense,
The goddess of light, and the goddess of scent.
The sun and the moon, the precious umbrella,
The banner of victory in every direction.
In the centre all treasures of both gods and men,
An excellent collection with nothing left out.
I offer this to all the Buddhas and Bodhisattvas, and
especially to you Avalokiteshvara, Buddha of
compassion;
Please accept with delight, for all migrating beings,
And having accepted, out of your great compassion
Please bestow your blessings on all sentient beings
pervading space.

The ground sprinkled with perfume and spread with
flowers,
The Great Mountain, four lands, sun and moon,
Seen as a Buddha Land and offered thus,
May all beings enjoy such Pure Lands.

I offer without any sense of loss
The objects that give rise to my attachment, hatred, and
confusion,
My friends, enemies, and strangers, our bodies and
enjoyments;
Please accept these and bless me to be released directly
from the three poisons.

IDAM GURU RATNA MANDALAKAM NIRYATAYAMI

Requesting the five great meanings

O Arya Avalokiteshvara, Treasure of Compassion,
And all your retinue, please listen to me.

Please quickly release me and all my mothers and
    fathers,
The six classes of living being, from the ocean of
    samsara.

Please generate quickly in our mental continuum
The vast and profound Dharma of the unsurpassed
    bodhichitta.

With your compassionate nectar please purify swiftly
The karma and delusion we have accumulated since
    beginningless time.

And with your hands of compassion please swiftly
    lead me
And all living beings to the Pure Land of Bliss.

O Amitabha and Avalokiteshvara,
Throughout all our lives please be our Spiritual Guide;
And by perfectly revealing the unmistaken path
Please lead us all swiftly to the state of Buddhahood.

Mantra recitation

As a result of these single-pointed requests,
Light rays radiate from Arya Avalokiteshvara's body
And purify all impure karmic appearances and mistaken
    awareness.
The environment becomes the Pure Land of Bliss,
And the body, speech, and mind of all the inhabitants
Transform into the body, speech, and mind of
    Avalokiteshvara.
All appearances, sounds, and conceptions become
    inseparable from emptiness.

OM MANI PÄME HUM   (100x or more)

The three recognitions

All the physical forms of myself and others are
   manifestations of Arya Avalokiteshvara's body,
All sounds are manifestations of the six-letter mantra,
And all mental activity arises from great exalted wisdom.

TRAINING IN THE ACTUAL POWA MEDITATION

Visualization

My body of light is translucent like a rainbow.
On my crown is Guru Avalokiteshvara, the synthesis of
   all Buddhas.
At his heart the Dharmakaya of all Buddhas
Appears as an oval-shaped jewel of white light, the size
   of a thumb.

In the centre of my body is my central channel,
Red and translucent, hollow and the width of an arrow.
Beginning four fingers below my navel, it widens as it
   ascends,
To join Avalokiteshvara's lower door at my crown.

At my heart inside the central channel is my mind,
A sparkling reddish-white drop, the size of a pea.
I, the drop, must attain liberation from samsara
By attaining the Pure Land of a Buddha.

The three awarenesses

My mind, the drop, is a traveller going to the Pure Land;
My central channel is the pathway;
The Dharmakaya of all Buddhas at Avalokiteshvara's
   heart is my destination.

Short mandala offering

The ground sprinkled with perfume and spread with
    flowers,
The Great Mountain, four lands, sun and moon,
Seen as a Buddha Land and offered thus,
May all beings enjoy such Pure Lands.

I offer without any sense of loss
The objects that give rise to my attachment, hatred, and
    confusion,
My friends, enemies, and strangers, our bodies and
    enjoyments;
Please accept these and bless me to be released directly
    from the three poisons.

IDAM GURU RATNA MANDALAKAM NIRYATAYAMI

Requests

O Guru Avalokiteshvara, synthesis of all direct and
    lineage Gurus,
I request you to dispel all my outer and inner obstacles.
Please bless me to complete the profound path of
    transference,
And lead me to the supreme Pure Land of Buddha.

O Guru Avalokiteshvara, synthesis of all Deities,
I request you to dispel all my outer and inner obstacles.
Please bless me to complete the profound path of
    transference,
And lead me to the supreme Pure Land of Buddha.

O Guru Avalokiteshvara, synthesis of all Buddha Jewels,
I request you to dispel all my outer and inner obstacles.
Please bless me to complete the profound path of
    transference,
And lead me to the supreme Pure Land of Buddha.

O Guru Avalokiteshvara, synthesis of all Dharma Jewels,
I request you to dispel all my outer and inner obstacles.
Please bless me to complete the profound path of
    transference,
And lead me to the supreme Pure Land of Buddha.

O Guru Avalokiteshvara, synthesis of all Sangha Jewels,
I request you to dispel all my outer and inner obstacles.
Please bless me to complete the profound path of
    transference,
And lead me to the supreme Pure Land of Buddha.

O Guru Avalokiteshvara, synthesis of all objects of
    refuge,
I request you to dispel all my outer and inner obstacles.
Please bless me to complete the profound path of
    transference,
And lead me to the supreme Pure Land of Buddha.

The actual meditation

Due to my single-pointed requests, from the oval-shaped
jewel of white light – the Dharmakaya of all Buddhas at
Avalokiteshvara's heart – a hook of white light descends
through my central channel and reaches the mind drop
at my heart. As it hooks my drop I draw my downward-
voiding wind upwards.

HIC
With my mind drop at my heart chakra poised to
ascend, like a bird about to fly, my body up to the
level of my heart dissolves into the drop.

HIC
As my mind drop ascends to the centre of my throat
chakra, my body up to the level of my throat dissolves
into the drop.

HIC
As my mind drop ascends to the centre of my crown chakra, the rest of my body dissolves into the drop.

My mind drop instantaneously enters the lower door of Avalokiteshvara and, reaching his heart, dissolves inseparably into the Dharmakaya of all Buddhas.

I experience the union of bliss and emptiness that is complete purity. I have reached the Pure Land of Buddha.

Meditate on this experience without distraction for as long as possible. You can complete three or seven rounds of this meditation in each session, from the visualization, 'My body of light is translucent like a rainbow . . . ', up to the end of the actual meditation.

Dedication

Realizing that the path begins with strong reliance
On my Spiritual Guide, the holy, supreme Field of Merit,
Through the force of our virtuous actions such as
    making offerings and prostrations
May I and all mother beings gain the realization of
    relying upon the Spiritual Guide.

Realizing that this precious human life, found only once,
Is difficult to attain, and yet decays so quickly,
May I seize its essential meaning,
Undistracted by the meaningless activities of this life.

Fearing the blazing fires of the sufferings of lower realms
From the depths of my heart I go for refuge to Buddha,
    Dharma, and Sangha.
May I strive sincerely
To abandon non-virtue and practise the entire collection
    of virtue.

Being violently tossed by the waves of delusion and karma
And tormented by the sea monsters of the three sufferings,
May I develop a strong wish for liberation
From the boundless and fearful great ocean of samsara.

Forsaking the mind that views as a pleasure garden
This unbearable prison of samsara,
May I take up the victory banner of liberation
By maintaining the three higher trainings and the
    wealths of Superiors.

Contemplating how all these pitiful migrators are my
    mothers,
Who out of kindness have cherished me again and again,
May I generate a spontaneous compassion
Like that of a loving mother for her dearest child.

In that no one wishes for even the slightest suffering,
Or is ever content with the happiness they have,
There is no difference between myself and others;
Realizing this, may I joyfully make others happy.

Seeing that this chronic disease of cherishing myself
Is the cause that gives rise to unwanted suffering,
May I destroy this great demon of selfishness
By resenting it as the object of blame.

Seeing that the mind that cherishes mother beings and
    would secure their happiness
Is the gateway that leads to infinite good qualities,
May I cherish these beings more than my life,
Even if they rise up against me as my enemies.

In short, since the childish are concerned for themselves
    alone,
Whereas Buddhas work solely for the sake of others,
May I distinguish the faults and benefits,
And thus be able to exchange myself with others.

Since cherishing myself is the door to all faults
And cherishing mother beings is the foundation of all
    good qualities,
May I take as my essential practice
The yoga of exchanging self with others.

Therefore, O Compassionate, Venerable Spiritual Guide,
May all the suffering, negativities, and obstructions of
    mother sentient beings
Ripen upon me right now;
And through my giving my happiness and virtue to
    others,
May all migrating beings be happy.

Though the world and its beings, filled with the effects
    of evil,
Pour down unwanted suffering like rain,
This is a chance to exhaust the effects of negative actions;
Seeing this, may I transform adverse conditions into the
    path.

In short, whether favourable or unfavourable conditions
    arise,
May I transform them into the path of improving the
    two bodhichittas
Through practising the five forces, the essence of all
    Dharmas,
And thereby maintain a happy mind alone.

May I make this precious human life extremely
    meaningful
By immediately applying meditation to whatever I meet
Through the skilful means of the four preparations,
And by practising the commitments and precepts of
    training the mind.

Through love, compassion, and superior intention,
And the magical practice of mounting taking and giving
   upon the breath,
May I generate the actual bodhichitta,
To free all migrators from this great ocean of samsara.

May I strive sincerely on the sole path
Traversed by all the Conquerors of the three times –
To bind my mind with pure Bodhisattva vows
And practise the three moral disciplines of the
   Mahayana.

May I complete the perfection of giving
Through the instructions on improving the mind of
   giving without attachment,
And thus transform my body, my enjoyments, and my
   virtues amassed throughout the three times
Into whatever each sentient being desires.

May I complete the perfection of moral discipline
By not transgressing even at the cost of my life
The discipline of the Pratimoksha, Bodhisattva, and
   Secret Mantra vows,
And by gathering virtuous Dharmas, and accomplishing
   the welfare of sentient beings.

May I complete the perfection of patience
So that even if every single being in the three realms,
Out of anger were to abuse me, criticize me, threaten
   me, or even take my life,
Undisturbed, I would repay their harm by helping them.

May I complete the perfection of effort
By striving for supreme enlightenment with unwavering
   compassion;
Even if I must remain in the fires of the deepest hell
For many aeons for the sake of each being.

May I complete the perfection of concentration
By abandoning the faults of mental sinking, mental
    excitement, and mental wandering,
And concentrating in single-pointed absorption
On the state that is the lack of true existence of all
    phenomena.

May I complete the perfection of wisdom
Through the yoga of the space-like meditative equipoise
    on the ultimate,
With the great bliss of the suppleness
Induced by the wisdom of individual analysis of thatness.

Outer and inner phenomena are like illusions, like
    dreams,
And like reflections of the moon in a clear lake,
For though they appear they do not truly exist;
Realizing this, may I complete the illusion-like
    concentration.

May I realize the meaning of Nagarjuna's intention,
That there is no contradiction but only harmony
Between the absence of even an atom of inherent
    existence in samsara and nirvana
And the non-deceptive dependent relationship of cause
    and effect.

And then the swirling ocean of the Tantras is crossed
Through the kindness of the navigator, the Vajra Holder.
May I cherish more than my life
The vows and commitments, the root of attainments.

Through the yoga of the first stage that transforms birth,
    death, and bardo,
Into the three bodies of the Conquerors,
May I purify all stains of ordinary appearance and
    conception,
And see whatever appears as the form of the Deity.

O Protector, please place your feet
On the centre of the eight-petalled lotus at my heart,
So that I may manifest within this life
The paths of illusory body, clear light, and union.

If by the time of my death I have not completed the path,
May I attain the Pure Land of Buddha
Through the instruction on correctly applying the five
   forces,
The supremely powerful method of transference to
   Buddhahood.   (3x)

In short, O Supreme Spiritual Guide, throughout all my
   lives
May I never be separated from you, but always come
   under your care;
And as the foremost of your disciples,
Maintain all the secrets of your body, speech, and mind.

O Supreme Spiritual Guide, wherever you manifest as a
   Buddha,
May I be the very first in your retinue;
And may everything be auspicious for me to accomplish
   without effort
All temporary and ultimate needs and wishes.

Due to my making requests in this way, O Supreme
   Spiritual Guide,
With delight, please come to my crown to bestow your
   blessings;
And once again firmly place your radiant feet
On the anthers of the lotus at my heart.

Colophon: This sadhana was compiled from traditional
sources by Venerable Geshe Kelsang Gyatso.

Path of Compassion for the Deceased

POWA SADHANA FOR THE BENEFIT
OF THE DECEASED

Introduction

To prepare for this ritual practice we begin by arranging offerings and other necessities. Whether the offerings are small or extensive will depend upon the amount dedicated by the relatives of the deceased. Using the money of the deceased person is a powerful method for increasing his or her merit, and for enabling him or her to make a special connection with the holy beings.

On a piece of paper we draw a lotus. In the centre of this we write in red ink the initial letter of the deceased's first name, and draw a canopy above it. We attach the paper to a stick to resemble a flag, and place this name-flag in a suitable container such as a small vase. In front of this we place a photograph or drawing of the deceased to symbolize his or her presence.

On a saucer we arrange a tablespoon of black sesame seeds in the shape of a scorpion, and we prepare a fire in a small container, preferably using charcoal. The name-flag, sesame seeds, and fire should be arranged on a table in front of our seat. Finally, we stand a small candle on a saucer in front of the photograph of the deceased.

Now with a mind of strong compassion for all sentient beings in general, and for the deceased in particular, we begin the sadhana.

Path of Compassion for the Deceased

SELF-GENERATION

Going for refuge and generating bodhichitta

I and all sentient beings, until we achieve enlightenment,
Go for refuge to Buddha, Dharma, and Sangha.
Through the virtues I collect by giving and other
    perfections,
May I become a Buddha for the benefit of all.   (3x)

Generating the four immeasurables

May everyone be happy,
May everyone be free from misery,
May no one ever be separated from their happiness,
May everyone have equanimity, free from hatred and
    attachment.

Self-generation as Avalokiteshvara

OM SÖBHAWA SHUDDHA SARWA DHARMA SÖBHAWA
    SHUDDHO HAM
Everything becomes emptiness.

From the state of emptiness, my mind arises as a white
letter HRIH standing on a white lotus and a moon
mandala. From this, lights radiate and perform the two
purposes. Gathering back, they completely transform,
and I arise as Arya Avalokiteshvara with a white-
coloured body, one face, and four hands.

The letter HRIH

My first two hands are pressed together at my heart holding a jewel, my lower right hand holds a crystal mala, and my lower left hand holds a white lotus flower. Ablaze with the signs and indications, I am adorned with jewelled ornaments and silk garments and sit in the vajra posture.

At my crown is an OM, at my throat is an AH, and at my heart is a HUM marked by a HRIH. From this, light rays radiate and invite from Potala Pure Land the wisdom beings, together with the empowering Deities.

DZA HUM BAM HO
We become non-dual.

The empowering Deities grant empowerment and my crown is adorned by Amitabha.

Offerings to the self-generation

OM ARYA LOKESHÖRA AHRGHAM PARTITZA HUM SÖHA
OM ARYA LOKESHÖRA PADÄM PARTITZA HUM SÖHA
OM ARYA LOKESHÖRA PUPE PARTITZA HUM SÖHA
OM ARYA LOKESHÖRA DHUPE PARTITZA HUM SÖHA
OM ARYA LOKESHÖRA ALOKE PARTITZA HUM SÖHA
OM ARYA LOKESHÖRA GÄNDHE PARTITZA HUM SÖHA
OM ARYA LOKESHÖRA NEWIDE PARTITZA HUM SÖHA
OM ARYA LOKESHÖRA SHAPTA PARTITZA HUM SÖHA

Praise

You whose white-coloured body is unstained by faults,
Whose crown is adorned with a fully enlightened
    Buddha,
Who gaze upon migrators with eyes of compassion,
To you Arya Avalokiteshvara I prostrate.

Mantra recitation

Light rays radiate from the letter HRIH at my heart
And purify all impure karmic appearances of living
  beings.
The environment becomes the Pure Land of Bliss,
And the body, speech, and mind of all the inhabitants
Transform into the body, speech, and mind of
  Avalokiteshvara.
All appearances, sounds, and conceptions become
  inseparable from the emptiness of the Dharmakaya.

OM MANI PÄME HUM

Recite as many as you wish.

Dedication

By this virtue may I quickly
Become Arya Avalokiteshvara,
And then lead every living being
Without exception to that ground.

THE ACTUAL PRACTICE

GENERATING THE DECEASED AS A LIVING PERSON

I am the Buddha of Compassion. Light rays radiate from
the letter HRIH at my heart and reach the symbolic form
of the deceased, which melts into light and becomes empty.

From the state of emptiness, [name of deceased] appears
in living aspect. His/her body is in the nature of light,
and his/her hands are folded in the gesture of prayer.

Again, light rays radiate from my heart throughout all
three realms, drawing back . . . 's consciousness, which
dissolves into the heart of the person generated in front.

PURIFYING THE NEGATIVE KARMA OF
THE DECEASED

Light rays radiate from the letter HRIH at my heart and reach the heart of the person generated in front. All his/her negative karmic imprints accumulated throughout countless lives leave through his/her nostrils in the form of countless tiny scorpions, which dissolve into the sesame seed scorpion.

The fire in front becomes empty.

From the state of emptiness, there appears a wisdom fire in the aspect of the enlightened Deity Vajradaka, who has a wide-open mouth.

OM VAJRA DAKA KHA KHA KHAHI KHAHI SARWA PAPAM DAHANA BHAKMI KURU SÖHA

While reciting the mantra, throw the sesame seeds – the nature of the deceased's negative karma – into the fire, and imagine that Vajradaka is consuming them. With each recitation of the mantra throw one pinch of sesame seeds into the fire using the thumb and ring finger of your right hand. After every seventh recitation, make the following heartfelt prayer:

May . . . be purified of all negativity,
May his/her outer and inner obstacles be pacified,
May he/she attain the Pure Land of a Buddha
And finally reach the pure Buddha grounds.

Continue in this way until all the sesame seeds have been burnt.

TRANSFERRING THE CONSCIOUSNESS OF THE
DECEASED TO THE PURE LAND

Visualization

. . . 's body of light is translucent like a rainbow.
On his/her crown is Guru Avalokiteshvara, the synthesis
of all Buddhas.
At Avalokiteshvara's heart the Dharmakaya of all
Buddhas
Appears as an oval-shaped jewel of white light, the size
of a thumb.

In the centre of . . . 's body is his/her central channel,
Red and translucent, hollow and the width of an arrow.
Beginning four fingers below his/her navel, it widens as
it ascends,
To join Avalokiteshvara's lower door at his/her crown.

At . . . 's heart inside his/her central channel is his/her
mind,
A sparkling reddish-white drop, the size of a pea.
May . . . attain liberation from samsara
By attaining the Pure Land of a Buddha.

The three awarenesses

. . . 's mind, the drop, is a traveller going to the Pure
Land;
His/her central channel is the pathway;
The Dharmakaya of all Buddhas at Avalokiteshvara's
heart is his/her destination.

*Focusing on Avalokiteshvara on the crown of the deceased,
make the following offerings and requests:*

Prayer of seven limbs

With my body, speech, and mind, humbly I prostrate,
And make offerings both set out and imagined.
I confess my wrong deeds from all time,
And rejoice in the virtues of all.
Please stay until samsara ceases,
And turn the Wheel of Dharma for us.
I dedicate all virtues to great enlightenment.

Short mandala offering

The ground sprinkled with perfume and spread with
    flowers,
The Great Mountain, four lands, sun and moon,
Seen as a Buddha Land and offered thus,
May all beings enjoy such Pure Lands.

I offer without any sense of loss
The objects that give rise to my attachment, hatred, and
    confusion,
My friends, enemies, and strangers, our bodies and
    enjoyments;
Please accept these and bless me to be released directly
    from the three poisons.

IDAM GURU RATNA MANDALAKAM NIRYATAYAMI

Requests

O Guru Avalokiteshvara, synthesis of all direct and
    lineage Gurus,
I request you to dispel all . . . 's outer and inner
    obstacles.
Please bless him/her to complete the profound path of
    transference,
And lead him/her to the supreme Pure Land of Buddha.

O Guru Avalokiteshvara, synthesis of all Deities,
I request you to dispel all . . . 's outer and inner
    obstacles.
Please bless him/her to complete the profound path of
    transference,
And lead him/her to the supreme Pure Land of Buddha.

O Guru Avalokiteshvara, synthesis of all Buddha Jewels,
I request you to dispel all . . . 's outer and inner
    obstacles.
Please bless him/her to complete the profound path of
    transference,
And lead him/her to the supreme Pure Land of Buddha.

O Guru Avalokiteshvara, synthesis of all Dharma Jewels,
I request you to dispel all . . . 's outer and inner
    obstacles.
Please bless him/her to complete the profound path of
    transference,
And lead him/her to the supreme Pure Land of Buddha.

O Guru Avalokiteshvara, synthesis of all Sangha Jewels,
I request you to dispel all . . . 's outer and inner
    obstacles.
Please bless him/her to complete the profound path of
    transference,
And lead him/her to the supreme Pure Land of Buddha.

O Guru Avalokiteshvara, synthesis of all objects of
    refuge,
I request you to dispel all . . . 's outer and inner
    obstacles.
Please bless him/her to complete the profound path of
    transference,
And lead him/her to the supreme Pure Land of Buddha.

The actual meditation

Due to my single-pointed requests, from the oval-shaped jewel of white light – the Dharmakaya of all Buddhas at Avalokiteshvara's heart – a hook of white light descends through . . . 's central channel and reaches the mind drop at his/her heart. As it hooks the drop, . . . 's downward-voiding wind is drawn upwards.

HIC
The mind drop ascends from the heart to the centre of the throat chakra.

HIC
The mind drop ascends to the centre of the crown chakra.

HIC
The mind drop instantaneously enters the lower door of Avalokiteshvara and, reaching his heart, dissolves inseparably into the Dharmakaya of all Buddhas.

. . . is now reborn in the Pure Land of Buddha.

Meditate on this conviction without distraction for as long as possible.

CONCLUSION

Having transferred the consciousness of the deceased to the Buddha Land, the imagined body in front dissolves into the letter on the name-flag.

Light the candle.

The candle is the nature of emptiness.

From the state of emptiness, there appears a five-coloured wisdom fire, the nature of the five Buddha families.

Burn the name-flag in the candle flame while chanting the mantra of Avalokiteshvara:

OM MANI PÄME HUM

As the wisdom fire burns, . . . 's body is purified,
And he/she attains a Buddha's Form Body.

Dedication

From the depths of your heart dedicate all your collection of virtue to the welfare of the deceased while concentrating on the meaning of the following prayer:

Through my great collection of virtue
May . . . realize all the stages of the path,
Attain the Pure Land of a Buddha,
And finally reach the Buddha grounds.   (3x)

Colophon: This sadhana was compiled from traditional sources by Venerable Geshe Kelsang Gyatso.

Path of Compassion
for the Dying

POWA SADHANA FOR THE BENEFIT
OF THE DYING

Introduction

When we know that someone is close to death we can practise powa on their behalf.

First we generate compassion by contemplating their suffering and how they have no choice over their next rebirth. Immediately after death they will experience the fears and suffering of the bardo. If they then take rebirth as a human being they will have to experience all the various human sufferings, if they are reborn as an animal they will have to experience the sufferings of an animal, and so forth. Contemplating their suffering, from the depths of our hearts we pray:

> *How wonderful it would be if this person were free from samsaric rebirth. I myself will make this happen.*

With this mind of compassion we then engage in this powa sadhana, *Path of Compassion for the Dying*, while deeply contemplating its meaning.

Generally, when someone is close to death it is very important not to touch any part of their body other than the crown. By touching their crown we shall cause the door of their crown chakra to open, and this will enable their consciousness to leave the body through the crown, thereby leading it to a higher rebirth. If the consciousness leaves through any of the lower doors of the body it will take rebirth in one of the lower realms. Understanding this is very important.

Also, while the dying person is still able to hear and understand what we are saying it is very important to keep their mind calm and peaceful, to encourage them, and to prevent them from becoming upset or unhappy. In this way they will die peacefully, without any disturbance.

If the dying person is a spiritual practitioner we can remind them of their daily practice, or at least recite or chant their daily prayers and mantras for them. We can also remind them of their Spiritual Guide in whom they have faith.

Path of Compassion for the Dying

SELF-GENERATION

Practise the self-generation of Avalokiteshvara, from going for refuge up to mantra recitation and dedication, by following Path of Compassion for the Deceased.

THE ACTUAL PRACTICE

IN-FRONT-GENERATION

I am the Buddha of Compassion. Light rays radiate from the letter HRIH at my heart and reach the dying person, who melts into light and becomes empty.

From the state of emptiness, [name of dying person] appears in front of me. His/her body is in the nature of light, and his/her hands are folded in the gesture of prayer.

TRANSFERRING THE CONSCIOUSNESS OF THE DYING PERSON TO THE PURE LAND

Visualization

. . . 's body of light is translucent like a rainbow.
On his/her crown is Guru Avalokiteshvara, the synthesis of all Buddhas.

At Avalokiteshvara's heart the Dharmakaya of all
 Buddhas
Appears as an oval-shaped jewel of white light, the size
 of a thumb.

In the centre of . . . 's body is his/her central channel,
Red and translucent, hollow and the width of an arrow.
Beginning four fingers below his/her navel, it widens as
 it ascends,
To join Avalokiteshvara's lower door at his/her crown.

At . . . 's heart inside his/her central channel is his/her
 mind,
A sparkling reddish-white drop, the size of a pea.
May . . . attain liberation from samsara
By attaining the Pure Land of a Buddha.

The three awarenesses

. . . 's mind, the drop, is a traveller going to the Pure
 Land;
His/her central channel is the pathway;
The Dharmakaya of all Buddhas at Avalokiteshvara's
 heart is his/her destination.

*Focusing on Avalokiteshvara on the crown of the dying
person in front of you, make the following offerings and
requests:*

Prayer of seven limbs

With my body, speech, and mind, humbly I prostrate,
And make offerings both set out and imagined.
I confess my wrong deeds from all time,
And rejoice in the virtues of all.
Please stay until samsara ceases,
And turn the Wheel of Dharma for us.
I dedicate all virtues to great enlightenment.

Short mandala offering

The ground sprinkled with perfume and spread with
    flowers,
The Great Mountain, four lands, sun and moon,
Seen as a Buddha Land and offered thus,
May all beings enjoy such Pure Lands.

I offer without any sense of loss
The objects that give rise to my attachment, hatred, and
    confusion,
My friends, enemies, and strangers, our bodies and
    enjoyments;
Please accept these and bless me to be released directly
    from the three poisons.

IDAM GURU RATNA MANDALAKAM NIRYATAYAMI

Requests

O Guru Avalokiteshvara, synthesis of all direct and
    lineage Gurus,
I request you to dispel all . . . 's outer and inner
    obstacles.
Please bless him/her to complete the profound path of
    transference,
And lead him/her to the supreme Pure Land of Buddha.

O Guru Avalokiteshvara, synthesis of all Deities,
I request you to dispel all . . . 's outer and inner
    obstacles.
Please bless him/her to complete the profound path of
    transference,
And lead him/her to the supreme Pure Land of Buddha.

O Guru Avalokiteshvara, synthesis of all Buddha Jewels,
I request you to dispel all . . . 's outer and inner
obstacles.
Please bless him/her to complete the profound path of
transference,
And lead him/her to the supreme Pure Land of Buddha.

O Guru Avalokiteshvara, synthesis of all Dharma Jewels,
I request you to dispel all . . . 's outer and inner
obstacles.
Please bless him/her to complete the profound path of
transference,
And lead him/her to the supreme Pure Land of Buddha.

O Guru Avalokiteshvara, synthesis of all Sangha Jewels,
I request you to dispel all . . . 's outer and inner
obstacles.
Please bless him/her to complete the profound path of
transference,
And lead him/her to the supreme Pure Land of Buddha.

O Guru Avalokiteshvara, synthesis of all objects of
refuge,
I request you to dispel all . . . 's outer and inner
obstacles.
Please bless him/her to complete the profound path of
transference,
And lead him/her to the supreme Pure Land of Buddha.

The actual meditation

Due to my single-pointed requests, from the oval-shaped
jewel of white light – the Dharmakaya of all Buddhas at
Avalokiteshvara's heart – a hook of white light descends
through . . . 's central channel and reaches the mind
drop at his/her heart. As it hooks the drop, . . . 's
downward-voiding wind is drawn upwards.

HIC

The mind drop ascends from the heart to the centre of
the throat chakra.

HIC

The mind drop ascends to the centre of the crown chakra.

HIC

The mind drop instantaneously enters the lower door
of Avalokiteshvara and, reaching his heart, dissolves
inseparably into the Dharmakaya of all Buddhas.

. . . is now reborn in the Pure Land of Buddha.

*Meditate on this conviction without distraction for as long
as possible.*

*From the depths of your heart dedicate all your collection
of virtue to the welfare of the dying person while concentrating on the meaning of the following prayer:*

Dedication

Through my great collection of virtue
May . . . realize all the stages of the path,
Attain the Pure Land of a Buddha,
And finally reach the Buddha grounds.   (3x)

Colophon: This sadhana was compiled from traditional
sources by Venerable Geshe Kelsang Gyatso.

Heartfelt Prayers

—————

FUNERAL SERVICE FOR CREMATIONS AND BURIALS

Introduction

If we are requested to perform a funeral rite for someone who has recently died, we can use this sadhana *Heartfelt Prayers*. This is a funeral service in which spiritual practitioners gather together to make heartfelt prayers and dedications for the deceased person to take a fortunate rebirth. Because it is a Buddhist service, the prayers are addressed to the assembly of Buddhas and other holy beings. The prayers set out in this ritual are only the basis for a funeral service, and may be adapted as appropriate.

The power of our prayers depends upon the strength and purity of our intention. In this service it is very important for everyone to have a mind of compassion for all living beings in general, and for the deceased in particular. If we have a genuinely compassionate motivation our prayers will definitely be effective.

Heartfelt Prayers

Preliminary prayers

In the space before me is the living Buddha Shakyamuni
surrounded by all the Buddhas and Bodhisattvas, like
the full moon surrounded by stars.

I and all sentient beings, until we achieve enlightenment,
Go for refuge to Buddha, Dharma, and Sangha.   (3x)

Through the virtues I collect by giving and other
   perfections,
May I become a Buddha for the benefit of all.   (3x)

May everyone be happy,
May everyone be free from misery,
May no one ever be separated from their happiness,
May everyone have equanimity, free from hatred and
   attachment.

Prayer of the Stages of the Path

The path begins with strong reliance
On my kind Teacher, source of all good;
O Bless me with this understanding
To follow him with great devotion.

This human life with all its freedoms,
Extremely rare, with so much meaning;
O Bless me with this understanding
All day and night to seize its essence.

My body, like a water bubble,
Decays and dies so very quickly;
After death come results of karma,
Just like the shadow of a body.

With this firm knowledge and remembrance
Bless me to be extremely cautious,
Always avoiding harmful actions
And gathering abundant virtue.

Samsara's pleasures are deceptive,
Give no contentment, only torment;
So please bless me to strive sincerely
To gain the bliss of perfect freedom.

O Bless me so that from this pure thought
Come mindfulness and greatest caution,
To keep as my essential practice
The doctrine's root, the Pratimoksha.

Just like myself all my kind mothers
Are drowning in samsara's ocean;
O So that I may soon release them,
Bless me to train in bodhichitta.

But I cannot become a Buddha
By this alone without three ethics;
So bless me with the strength to practise
The Bodhisattva's ordination.

By pacifying my distractions
And analyzing perfect meanings,
Bless me to quickly gain the union
Of special insight and quiescence.

When I become a pure container
Through common paths, bless me to enter
The essence practice of good fortune,
The supreme vehicle, Vajrayana.

The two attainments both depend on
My sacred vows and my commitments;
Bless me to understand this clearly
And keep them at the cost of my life.

By constant practice in four sessions,
The way explained by holy Teachers,
O Bless me to gain both the stages,
Which are the essence of the Tantras.

May those who guide me on the good path,
And my companions all have long lives;
Bless me to pacify completely
All obstacles, outer and inner.

May I always find perfect Teachers,
And take delight in holy Dharma,
Accomplish all grounds and paths swiftly,
And gain the state of Vajradhara.

From the hearts of all the holy beings, streams of light
and nectar flow down, blessing and purifying . . . 's
mind.

The assembly observes a short period of silence.

Remembrance

A remembrance of the deceased is delivered.

The officiant leads the assembly in prayer:

Buddha taught that all life is impermanent and that all
those who are born must eventually pass from this life.
However, everyone has within them the seeds of their
past virtues, which have the power to bring a fortunate
rebirth in the future.

We pray that through the power of this virtue, through
the blessings of the holy beings, and through the force

of our heartfelt prayers, our dear friend, . . . , will experience great good fortune and everlasting peace and happiness.

We also pray for the bereaved relatives and friends, that they may be comforted in their loss and find peace of mind and strength of heart.

May all beings without exception be released from suffering, and find true happiness and everlasting peace.

Additional prayers can be recited at this point.

The assembly observes a few moments of silent contemplation and prayer.

Now, while focusing strongly on compassion for all living beings in general and for the deceased in particular, the assembly chants the mantra of the Buddha of Compassion twenty-one times:

OM MANI PÄME HUM

Dedication prayers

The officiant says:

We now dedicate all the virtues we have collected to the future happiness of our dear friend . . . .

The assembly recites the following prayers:

Through the virtues we have collected
By practising the stages of the path,
May . . . find the opportunity
To practise in the same way.

May . . . experience
The happiness of humans and gods,
And quickly attain enlightenment,
So that his/her samsara is finally extinguished.

May there arise in . . . 's mind
Great faith in Buddha, Dharma, and Sangha,
And thus may he/she always receive
The blessings of the Three Precious Jewels.

May . . . meet precious Teachers
Who reveal the stages of the path to enlightenment,
And through engaging in this path
May he/she quickly attain the ultimate peace of full
   enlightenment.

The Buddhadharma is the supreme medicine
That relieves all mental pain,
So may this precious Dharma Jewel
Pervade all worlds throughout space.

However many living beings there are
Experiencing mental and physical suffering,
May their suffering cease through the power of our
   merit,
And may they find everlasting happiness and joy.

May there never arise in this world
The miseries of incurable disease, famine, or war,
Or the dangers of earthquakes, fires,
Floods, storms, and so forth.

Through the blessings of the Buddhas and Bodhisattvas,
The truth of actions and their effects,
And the power of our pure superior intention,
May all our prayers be fulfilled.

Colophon: This sadhana was compiled from traditional
sources by Venerable Geshe Kelsang Gyatso.

Mahayana Confession Sutra

SUTRA OF THE THREE SUPERIOR HEAPS

Introduction

In our previous lives, while under the influence of deluded minds, we created a great deal of negative karma, and we also transgressed our commitments and incurred root and secondary downfalls. As a result we now experience difficulties in developing faith and conviction in Dharma, and in making progress on the stages of the path to enlightenment. Moreover, if we do not purify all this negativity while we have the chance we shall have to experience great suffering in the future.

Any living being, even a worm or an insect, can commit negative actions, but only humans have the fortune to be able to purify them. We have been accumulating non-virtuous actions and experiencing their suffering results since beginningless time, but we now have the opportunity to purify them completely. We should make use of this precious opportunity to purify our negative karma, not to create more! Since purification is the root of future happiness and spiritual realizations we should strive to cleanse our mind of delusions and negative karma. One of the best methods for purifying negativities and downfalls is the *Mahayana Confession Sutra*, otherwise known as the *Sutra of the Three Superior Heaps*, or *The Bodhisattva's Confession of Moral Downfalls*.

Mahayana Confession Sutra

Namo: *The Bodhisattva's Confession of Moral Downfalls*

I, whose name is . . . , at all times go for refuge to the Guru, go for refuge to the Buddha, go for refuge to the Dharma, go for refuge to the Sangha.

To the Teacher, Blessed One, Tathagata, Foe Destroyer, Completely Perfect Buddha, Glorious Conqueror Shakyamuni I prostrate.

To the Tathagata Complete Subduer with the Essence of Vajra I prostrate.

To the Tathagata Jewel of Radiant Light I prostrate.

To the Tathagata Powerful King of the Nagas I prostrate.

To the Tathagata Leader of the Heroes I prostrate.

To the Tathagata Glorious Pleasure I prostrate.

To the Tathagata Jewel Fire I prostrate.

To the Tathagata Jewel Moonlight I prostrate.

To the Tathagata Meaningful to Behold I prostrate.

To the Tathagata Jewel Moon I prostrate.

To the Tathagata Stainless One I prostrate.

To the Tathagata Bestower of Glory I prostrate.

To the Tathagata Pure One I prostrate.

To the Tathagata Transforming with Purity I prostrate.

To the Tathagata Water Deity I prostrate.

To the Tathagata God of Water Deities I prostrate.

To the Tathagata Glorious Excellence I prostrate.

To the Tathagata Glorious Sandalwood I prostrate.

To the Tathagata Endless Splendour I prostrate.

To the Tathagata Glorious Light I prostrate.

To the Tathagata Glorious One without Sorrow
I prostrate.

To the Tathagata Son without Craving I prostrate.

To the Tathagata Glorious Flower I prostrate.

To the Tathagata Clearly Knowing through Enjoying
Pure Radiance I prostrate.

To the Tathagata Clearly Knowing through Enjoying
Lotus Radiance I prostrate.

To the Tathagata Glorious Wealth I prostrate.

To the Tathagata Glorious Mindfulness I prostrate.

To the Tathagata Glorious Name of Great Renown
I prostrate.

To the Tathagata King of the Victory Banner, Head
of the Powerful Ones I prostrate.

To the Tathagata Glorious One Complete Subduer
I prostrate.

To the Tathagata Great Victor in Battle I prostrate.

To the Tathagata Glorious One Complete Subduer
Passed Beyond I prostrate.

To the Tathagata Glorious Array Illuminating All
I prostrate.

To the Tathagata Jewel Lotus Great Subduer I prostrate.

To the Tathagata, Foe Destroyer, Completely Perfect
  Buddha, King of Mount Meru Seated Firmly on a
  Jewel and a Lotus I prostrate.

O All you [Tathagatas] and all the others, however many
Tathagatas, the Foe Destroyers, the Completely Perfect
Buddhas, the Blessed Ones there are dwelling and abiding
in all the worldly realms of the ten directions, all you
Buddhas, the Blessed Ones, please listen to me.

In this life and in all my lives since beginningless time,
in all my places of rebirth whilst wandering in samsara, I
have done negative actions, have ordered them to be done,
and have rejoiced in their being done. I have stolen the property of the bases of offering, the property of the Sangha,
and the property of the Sanghas of the ten directions, have
ordered it to be stolen, and have rejoiced in it being stolen.
I have committed the five unbounded heinous actions, have
ordered them to be committed, and have rejoiced in their
being committed. I have completely engaged in the paths
of the ten non-virtuous actions, have ordered others to
engage in them, and have rejoiced in their engaging in
them.

Being obstructed by such karmic obstructions, I shall
become a hell being, or I shall be born as an animal, or I
shall go to the land of the hungry spirits, or I shall be born
as a barbarian in an irreligious country, or I shall be born
as a long-life god, or I shall come to have incomplete senses, or I shall come to hold wrong views, or I shall have no
opportunity to please a Buddha.

All such karmic obstructions I declare in the presence of
the Buddhas, the Blessed Ones, who have become exalted
wisdom, who have become 'eyes', who have become wit-
nesses, who have become valid, who see with their wisdom. I confess without concealing or hiding anything, and
from now on I shall avoid and refrain from such actions.

All you Buddhas, the Blessed Ones, please listen to me. In this life and in all my previous lives since beginningless time, in all my places of rebirth whilst wandering in samsara, whatever root of virtue there is in my giving to others, even in my giving a morsel of food to one born as an animal; whatever root of virtue there is in my maintaining moral discipline; whatever root of virtue there is in my actions conducive to great liberation; whatever root of virtue there is in my acting to fully ripen sentient beings; whatever root of virtue there is in my generating a supreme mind of enlightenment; and whatever root of virtue there is in my unsurpassed exalted wisdom; all of these assembled, gathered, and collected together, by fully dedicating them to the unsurpassed, to that of which there is no higher, to that which is even higher than the high, and to that which surpasses the unsurpassed, I fully dedicate to the unsurpassed, perfect, complete enlightenment.

Just as the Buddhas, the Blessed Ones of the past, have dedicated fully, just as the Buddhas, the Blessed Ones who are yet to come, will dedicate fully, and just as the Buddhas, the Blessed Ones who are living now, dedicate fully, so too do I dedicate fully.

I confess individually all negative actions. I rejoice in all merit. I beseech and request all the Buddhas. May I attain the holy, supreme, unsurpassed, exalted wisdom.

Whoever are the Conquerors, the supreme beings living now, those of the past, and likewise those who are yet to come, with a boundless ocean of praise for all your good qualities, and with my palms pressed together I go close to you for refuge.

This concludes the Mahayana Sutra entitled *Sutra of the Three Superior Heaps*.

Glossary

Basis of imputation All phenomena are imputed upon their parts, therefore any of the individual parts, or the entire collection of the parts, of any phenomenon is its basis of imputation. A phenomenon is imputed by mind in dependence upon its basis of imputation appearing to that mind. See *Heart of Wisdom*.

Beginningless time According to the Buddhist world view there is no beginning to mind, and so no beginning to time. Therefore, all sentient beings have taken countless previous rebirths.

Blessings (Tib. jin gyi lab pa) The transformation of our mind from a negative state to a positive state, from an unhappy state to a happy state, or from a state of weakness to a state of strength, through the inspiration of holy beings such as our Spiritual Guide, Buddhas, and Bodhisattvas.

Buddha family There are five main Buddha families: the families of Vairochana, Ratnasambhava, Amitabha, Amoghasiddhi, and Akshobya. They are the five purified aggregates – the aggregates of form, feeling, discrimination, compositional factors, and consciousness, respectively; and the five exalted wisdoms – the exalted mirror-like wisdom, the exalted wisdom of equality, the exalted wisdom of individual realization, the exalted wisdom of accomplishing activities, and the exalted wisdom of the Dharmadhatu, respectively. See *Great Treasury of Merit*.

Buddha nature See Buddha seed.

Buddha's bodies A Buddha has four bodies – the Wisdom Truth Body, the Nature Body, the Enjoyment Body, and the Emanation Body. The first is Buddha's omniscient mind; the second is the emptiness, or ultimate nature, of his mind; the third is his subtle Form Body; and the fourth, of which each Buddha manifests a countless number, are gross Form Bodies that are visible to ordinary beings. The Wisdom Truth Body and the Nature Body are both included within the Truth Body, and the Enjoyment Body and the Emanation Body are both included within the Form Body. See *Joyful Path of Good Fortune*.

Buddha seed The root mind of a sentient being, and its ultimate nature. Buddha seed, Buddha nature, and Buddha lineage are synonyms.

Central channel The principal channel at the very centre of the body along which the chakras, or channel wheels, are located. See *Clear Light of Bliss*.

Chakra Sanskrit for 'channel wheel'. A focal centre where secondary channels branch out from the central channel. Meditating on these points can cause the inner winds to enter the central channel. See *Clear Light of Bliss*.

Chakravatin king An extremely fortunate being who has accumulated a vast amount of merit and as a result has taken rebirth as a king with dominion over all four continents, or at the very least over one of the four continents. At present there are no chakravatin kings in our world, and there is no one who has complete dominion over our continent, Jambudipa. See *Great Treasury of Merit*.

Chittamatra The lower of the two schools of Mahayana tenets. 'Chittamatra' means 'mind only'. According to this school all phenomena are the same nature as the mind that apprehends them. They also assert that dependent phenomena are truly existent but do not exist external to the mind. A Chittamatrin is a proponent of Chittamatra tenets. See *Meaningful to Behold* and *Ocean of Nectar*.

Clear light A manifest very subtle mind that perceives an appearance like clear, empty space. See *Clear Light of Bliss* and *Tantric Grounds and Paths*.

Collective karma The karma we create when we act in association with others. Those who create karma together also experience its effects together.

Conceptual mind A thought that apprehends its object through a generic image. See *Understanding the Mind*.

222

Conventional truth Any phenomenon other than emptiness. Conventional truths are true with respect to the minds of ordinary beings, but in reality they are false. See *Heart of Wisdom*.

Degenerate times A period when spiritual activity degenerates.

Deity (Skt. Yidam) A Tantric enlightened being.

Desire realm The environment of hell beings, hungry spirits, animals, humans, demi-gods, and the gods who enjoy the five objects of desire.

Divine pride A non-deluded pride that regards oneself as a Deity and one's environment and enjoyments as those of the Deity. It is the antidote to ordinary conceptions. See *Guide to Dakini Land*.

Emanation Animate or inanimate form manifested by Buddhas or high Bodhisattvas to benefit others.

Four noble truths True sufferings, true origins, true cessations, and true paths. They are called 'noble' truths because they are supreme objects of meditation. Through meditation on these four objects we can realize ultimate truth directly and thus become a noble, or Superior, being. See *Joyful Path of Good Fortune*.

Generic image The appearing object of a conceptual mind. See *Heart of Wisdom* and *Understanding the Mind*.

Geshe A title given by the Kadampa monasteries to accomplished Buddhist scholars.

Hearer One of two types of Hinayana practitioner. Both Hearers and Solitary Realizers are Hinayanists but they differ in their motivation, behaviour, merit, and wisdom. In all these respects Solitary Realizers are superior to Hearers.

Hinayana Sanskrit word for 'Lesser Vehicle'. The Hinayana goal is to attain merely one's own liberation from suffering by completely abandoning delusions. See *Joyful Path of Good Fortune*.

Imprints There are two types of imprint: imprints of actions and imprints of delusions. Every action leaves an imprint on the mind. These imprints are karmic potentialities to experience certain effects in the future. Imprints of delusions remain even after the delusions themselves have been abandoned. They are obstructions to omniscience, and are completely abandoned only by Buddhas.

Indestructible drop The most subtle drop, which is located at the heart. It is formed from the essence of the white and red drops received from our parents at conception. See *Tantric Grounds and Paths* and *Clear Light of Bliss*.

Inner winds Special winds related to the mind that flow through the channels of our body. Our body and mind cannot function without these winds. See *Clear Light of Bliss*.

Kadampa A Tibetan word in which 'Ka' means all Buddha's teachings, 'dam' the special arrangement of Lamrim presented by Atisha, and 'pa' a person who integrates all the teachings of Buddha that they know into their Lamrim practice.

Lamrim Literally, 'stages of the path'. A special arrangement of all Buddha's teachings that is easy to understand and put into practice. It reveals all the stages of the path to enlightenment. See *Joyful Path of Good Fortune* and *The Meditation Handbook*.

Madhyamika The higher of the two schools of Mahayana tenets. The Madhyamika view was taught by Buddha in the *Perfection of Wisdom Sutras* during the second turning of the Wheel of Dharma and was subsequently elucidated by Nagarjuna and his followers. There are two divisions of this school, Madhyamika-Svatantrika and Madhyamika-Prasangika, of which the latter is Buddha's final view. See *Meaningful to Behold* and *Ocean of Nectar*.

Mahasiddha Sanskrit word for 'Greatly Accomplished One', which is used to refer to Yogis and Yoginis with high attainments.

Mara Anything that obstructs the attainment of liberation or enlightenment. There are four principal types of mara: the mara of the delusions, the mara of contaminated aggregates, the mara of uncontrolled death, and the Devaputra mara. Of these, only the last are actual sentient beings. See *Heart of Wisdom*.

Mental factor A cognizer that principally apprehends a particular attribute of an object. There are fifty-one specific mental factors. See also *Primary mind*. See *Understanding the Mind*.

Obstructions to liberation Obstructions that prevent the attainment of liberation. All delusions, such as ignorance, attachment, and anger, together with their seeds, are obstructions to liberation. Also called 'delusion-obstructions'.

Obstructions to omniscience The imprints of delusions that prevent simultaneous and direct realization of all phenomena. Only Buddhas have overcome these obstructions.

Ordinary being Anyone who has not realized emptiness directly.

Pratimoksha Sanskrit word for 'individual liberation'. See *The Bodhisattva Vow*.

Primary mind A cognizer that principally apprehends the mere entity of an object. There are six primary minds: eye consciousness, ear consciousness, nose consciousness, tongue consciousness, body consciousness, and mental consciousness. Each moment of mind comprises a primary mind and various mental factors. A primary mind and its accompanying mental factors are the same entity but have different functions. See *Understanding the Mind*.

Sadhana (Tib. drub thab) A ritual that is a method for attaining spiritual realizations. It can be associated with Sutra or Tantra.

Secret Mantra Synonymous with Tantra. Secret Mantra teachinngs are distinguished from Sutra teachings in that they reveal methods for training the mind by bringing the future result, or Buddhahood, into the present path. Secret Mantra is the supreme path to full enlightenment. The term 'Mantra' indicates that it is Buddha's special instruction for protecting our mind from ordinary appearances and conceptions. Practitioners of Secret Mantra overcome ordinary appearances and conceptions by visualizing their body, environment, enjoyments, and deeds as those of a Buddha. The term 'Secret' indicates that the practices are to be done in private, and that they can be practised only by those who have received a Tantric empowerment. See *Tantric Grounds and Paths*.

Sense power An inner power located in the very centre of a sense organ that functions directly to produce a sense awareness. There are five sense powers, one for each type of sense awareness – the eye awareness and so forth. See *Understanding the Mind*.

Shantideva (AD 687-763) A great Indian Buddhist scholar and meditation master. See *Meaningful to Behold*.

Signs of dissolution Internal signs that the inner winds are dissolving within the central channel. See *Clear Light of Bliss*.

Six perfections The perfections of giving, moral discipline, patience, effort, mental stabilization, and wisdom. They are called 'perfections' because they are motivated by bodhichitta. See *Joyful Path of Good Fortune*.

Solitary Realizer See *Hearer*.

Superior being (Skt. Arya) A being who has a direct realization of emptiness.

Sutras The teachings of Buddha that are open to everyone to practise without the need for empowerment. These include Buddha's teachings of the three turnings of the Wheel of Dharma.

Tantra See *Secret Mantra*.

Three higher trainings Training in moral discipline, concentration, and wisdom motivated by renunciation or bodhichitta.

Three realms The three levels within samsara: the desire realm, the form realm, and the formless realm. Beings of the desire realm have powerful delusions, beings of the form realm have more subtle delusions, and beings of the formless realm have very subtle delusions. See also *Desire realm*.

View of the transitory collection A type of self-grasping of persons that grasps one's own I as being an inherently existent I. See *Joyful Path of Good Fortune*.

Wrong awareness A cognizer that is mistaken with respect to its engaged object. See *Understanding the Mind*.

Wrong view An intellectually-formed wrong awareness that denies the existence of an object that it is necessary to understand to attain liberation or enlightenment – for example, denying the existence of enlightened beings, karma, or rebirth. See *Joyful Path of Good Fortune*.

Yoga A term used for various spiritual practices that entail maintaining a special view, such as Guru yoga and the yogas of eating, sleeping, dreaming, and waking. 'Yoga' also refers to union, such as the union of tranquil abiding and superior seeing.

Yogi or Yogini The Sanskrit word 'Yogi' usually refers to someone who has attained the union of tranquil abiding and superior seeing.

Bibliography

Geshe Kelsang Gyatso is a highly respected meditation master and scholar of the Mahayana Buddhist tradition founded by Je Tsongkhapa. Since arriving in the UK in 1977, Geshe Kelsang has worked tirelessly to establish pure Buddhadharma throughout the world. Over this period he has given extensive teachings on the major scriptures of the Mahayana. These teachings are currently being published and provide a comprehensive presentation of the essential Sutra and Tantra practices of Mahayana Buddhism.

Books in print

The following books by Geshe Kelsang are all published by Tharpa Publications.

The Bodhisattva Vow. The essential practices of Mahayana Buddhism. (2nd. edn., 1995)
Buddhism: A Beginner's Guide. (2000)
Clear Light of Bliss. The practice of Mahamudra in Vajrayana Buddhism. (2nd. edn., 1992)
Essence of Vajrayana. The Highest Yoga Tantra practice of Heruka body mandala. (1997)
Great Treasury of Merit. The practice of relying upon a Spiritual Guide. (1992)
Guide to Dakini Land. The Highest Yoga Tantra practice of Buddha Vajrayogini. (2nd. edn., 1996)
Heart Jewel. The essential practices of Kadampa Buddhism. (2nd. edn., 1997)
Heart of Wisdom. The essential wisdom teachings of Buddha. (3rd. edn., 1996)
Introduction to Buddhism. An explanation of the Buddhist way of life. (2nd. edn., 1995)
Joyful Path of Good Fortune. The complete Buddhist path to enlightenment. (2nd. edn., 1996)

Living Meaningfully, Dying Joyfully. The profound practice of
transference of consciousness. (1999)

Meaningful to Behold. The Bodhisattva's way of life.
(4th. edn., 1994)

The Meditation Handbook. A practical guide to Buddhist meditation.
(3rd. edn., 1995)

Ocean of Nectar. Wisdom and compassion in Mahayana Buddhism.
(1995)

Tantric Grounds and Paths. How to enter, progress on, and
complete the Vajrayana path. (1994)

Understanding the Mind. An explanation of the nature and
functions of the mind. (2nd. edn., 1997)

Universal Compassion. Transforming your life through love and
compassion. (3rd. edn., 1997)

Sadhanas

Geshe Kelsang has also supervised the translation of a collection of
essential sadhanas, or prayer booklets. Those in print include:

Assembly of Good Fortune. The tsog offering for Heruka body
mandala.

Avalokiteshvara Sadhana. Prayers and requests to the Buddha of
Compassion.

The Bodhisattva's Confession of Moral Downfalls. The purification
practice of the *Mahayana Sutra of the Three Superior Heaps*.

Condensed Essence of Vajrayana. Condensed Heruka body mandala
self-generation sadhana.

Dakini Yoga. Six-session Guru yoga combined with self-generation
as Vajrayogini.

Drop of Essential Nectar. A special fasting and purification practice
in conjunction with Eleven-faced Avalokiteshvara.

Essence of Good Fortune. Prayers for the six preparatory practices
for meditation on the stages of the path to enlightenment.

Essence of Vajrayana. Heruka body mandala self-generation
sadhana according to the system of Mahasiddha Ghantapa.

Feast of Great Bliss. Vajrayogini self-initiation sadhana.

Great Compassionate Mother. The sadhana of Arya Tara.

Great Liberation of the Mother. Preliminary prayers for Mahamudra
meditation in conjunction with Vajrayogini practice.

The Great Mother. A method to overcome hindrances and obstacles
by reciting the *Essence of Wisdom Sutra* (the *Heart Sutra*).

Heartfelt Prayers. Funeral service for cremations and burials.

Heart Jewel. The Guru yoga of Je Tsongkhapa combined with the condensed sadhana of his Dharma Protector.

The Hundreds of Deities of the Joyful Land. The Guru yoga of Je Tsongkhapa.

The Kadampa Way of Life. Essential practices of the New Kadampa Tradition.

Liberation from Sorrow. Praises and requests to the Twenty-one Taras.

Mahayana Refuge Ceremony and Bodhisattva Vow Ceremony.

Medicine Guru Sadhana. The method for making requests to the Assembly of Seven Medicine Buddhas.

Meditation and Recitation of Solitary Vajrasattva.

Melodious Drum Victorious in all Directions. The extensive fulfilling and restoring ritual of the Dharma Protector, the great king Dorje Shugdän, in conjunction with Mahakala, Kalarupa, Kalindewi, and other Dharma Protectors.

Offering to the Spiritual Guide (*Lama Chöpa*). A special Guru yoga practice of Je Tsongkhapa's tradition.

Prayers for Meditation. Brief preparatory prayers for meditation.

A Pure Life. The practice of taking and keeping the eight Mahayana precepts.

The Quick Path. A condensed practice of Heruka Five Deities according to Master Ghantapa's tradition.

Quick Path to Great Bliss. Vajrayogini self-generation sadhana.

Treasury of Blessings. The condensed meaning of Vajrayana Mahamudra and prayers of request to the lineage Gurus.

Treasury of Wisdom. The sadhana of Venerable Manjushri.

Vajra Hero Yoga. A brief essential practice of Heruka body mandala self-generation, and condensed six-session yoga.

Wishfulfilling Jewel. The Guru yoga of Je Tsongkhapa combined with the sadhana of his Dharma Protector.

The Yoga of Buddha Amitayus. A special method for increasing life span, wisdom, and merit.

For a catalogue of all our publications please contact:

Tharpa Publications
Kilnwick Percy Hall
Pocklington
York YO42 1UF, England

Tel: 01759-306446   Fax: 01759-306397

E-mail: tharpa@tharpa.com
Website: www.tharpa.com

- NKT -

Study Programmes

Geshe Kelsang has prepared three study programmes based on his books, which are designed to fulfil the wishes of those who would like to study Buddhism systematically and thereby deepen their experience of the essential practices.

The **General Programme** provides a basic introduction to Buddhist view, meditation, and action, and various kinds of teaching and practice from both Sutra and Tantra.

The **Foundation Programme** is designed for those who prefer a more structured approach to their spiritual training. Based on five of Geshe Kelsang's books, this programme lasts for approximately four years. The classes consist of readings, teachings, discussion, pujas, and meditations. It is possible to enrol for one subject at a time. Each subject concludes with an examination.

The **Teacher Training Programme** is designed for those who wish to train as authentic Dharma Teachers. This programme, which takes approximately seven years to complete, is based on twelve of Geshe Kelsang's books. To qualify as Dharma Teachers, participants must complete the study of all twelve texts, pass an examination in each subject, satisfy certain criteria with regard to behaviour and life style, and complete various meditation retreats.

These three programmes are taught worldwide at Centres of the New Kadampa Tradition. All these Centres are under the spiritual direction of Geshe Kelsang. Their addresses are available from:

James Belither ~ Secretary
New Kadampa Tradition (NKT)
Conishead Priory
Ulverston
Cumbria LA12 9QQ, England

Tel/Fax: 01229-588533

E-mail: kadampa@dircon.co.uk
Website: www.kadampa.com

Index

helping those who have died
    12, 49, 71-83
Heruka 12, 23, 37, 113
HIC 36, 78, 79
higher rebirth 3
    causes of 5, 84, 97, 147-8
Highest Yoga Tantra 71, 113
Hinayana 100-1, g
HRIH 14
human rebirth (see also precious
    human life) 37, 68-9, 147-8
    sufferings of 105-6, 139,
    148

I (see also self-grasping, of
    persons) 33, 106, 108-10
ignorance (see also self-grasping)
    105, 129, 137
    sleep of 5
    types of 129
illness (see sickness)
impermanence 50, 53, 63, 115
    subtle 131
imprints 3, 5, 117, 144, g
imputation 33, 106, 107, 140
inappropriate attention 119,
    122, 139
indestructible drop 46, g
Indra 19
inherent existence 107-8
inner winds 6, 45-6, 64, g
    life-supporting 41
intention 30, 80, 102, 148, 152
intermediate state (see also
    bardo beings) 6, 64-8

Je Tsongkhapa 25, 142-3
Joyful Path of Good Fortune 123,
    152

Kadampa g
    Geshe 82, 148
    Teachers 3

karma (see also actions and effects;
    non-virtuous actions; virtuous
    actions) 54, 129, 147-8
    collective 50, g
    contaminated 105
    throwing 69, 132
karmic connections 12, 23
karmic obstructions 142
Kashyapa 20
Keajra 37
Khädrubje 142-3
killing 139, 148, 149
kindness 45, 103-5, 125
Kushinagar 50

Lamrim (see also stages of the
    path) 82, 91, g
laziness 29-30, 88, 111, 113-5,
    117-8
Lhogo 71
liberation 89, 90, 100, 115
    cause of 14, 17, 110
    great 19, 89, 145
    three levels 89
life force 39, 41, 56
life span 37, 39-41, 42, 53, 57
    of bardo being 65-6
life-supporting wind 41
listening 95, 116
Little Sambara Tantra 11
living beings 104
Longdöl Lama 3-4, 47
love 28, 101-5
    three types 102, 105
lower rebirth 66, 68
    causes of 5, 18, 124, 147-8
    protection from 97, 149

Madhyamika 24, g
Mahakashyapa 50
Mahasiddha 11, g
Mahayana Confession Sutra 150,
    152

234